PASTORAL ETHICS

PASTORAL ETHICS

Professional Responsibilities of the Clergy

GAYLORD NOYCE

ABINGDON PRESS
Nashville

PASTORAL ETHICS

This book is printed on acid-free paper.

Library of Congress Cataloging-in-Publication Data

Noyce, Gaylord B.
　Pastoral ethics.

　Bibliography: p.
　Includes index.
　1. Clergy—Professional ethics. I. Title.
　BV4011.5.N69　　　1988　　　241'.641　　　87-19302
　　　　　　ISBN 0-687-30338-9
　　　　　　　(alk. paper)

Scripture quotations in this publication are from the Revised Standard
Version of the Bible, copyrighted 1946, 1952, © 1971, 1973 by the Division of
Christian Education of the National Council of the Churches of Christ in the
U.S.A., and are used by permission.

MANUFACTURED BY THE PARTHENON PRESS AT
NASHVILLE, TENNESSEE, UNITED STATES OF AMERICA

For Harper and Julia Welch

CONTENTS

INTRODUCTION

There is special warrant these days for examining our ministry through the lens of professional ethics. Much of the general work on pastoral ethics is now out of print and almost quaint in style and content.

More importantly, professional ethics contributes to clarifying professional identity. We urgently need that clarity at present. H. Richard Niebuhr called the ministry of his generation a "perplexed profession." The situation is hardly improved. Clergy "burnout," so publicized, results more from a blurred pastoral identity than from overwork. Professional ethics well taught counteracts that kind of haziness.

Not long ago, two seminary faculty members asked recent graduates of their school to reflect on their theological education. To their dismay, the researchers found that the major concern of these pastors was not complementing their academic experience with more on-the-job skills. Rather it was coping with their uncertainties as to who they were in ministry. "We found beginning clergypersons almost completely at the mercy of the expectations of their first parish without counterbalancing claims from denomination or profession. Formation of clerical identity depended on satisfying this first congregation."[1] The writers put their

11

surprise in these words: "We suddenly found ourselves dealing with a profession with no canons of good practice, and consequently no supervision by professional peers to inculcate them. It would be difficult to sue a minister for malpractice, with bona fide practice so ill-defined. . . . [T]here seem to be no commonly accepted canons for integrity in the practice of ministry."[2]

It would be appealing to diagnose the problems of these pastors as caused by deficient theological perspective or faulty spirituality. Undoubtedly such a diagnosis is on target. However, to enable the pastors to capture a sense of their rootage in a certain tradition of work and service may be of even more immediate and practical help to them. They have a defined social role, one with professional guidelines and norms. Restrictive as "professional" structuring of life may seem to some, it is liberating for those who, while having most of the right instincts and ideals, still flounder as these young clergy evidently do. An ethics of professional ministry will contribute to their self-understanding. Moreover, it will undergird freedom and creativity far better than does a debilitating puzzlement at what in God's name a pastor is supposed to be doing when a congregation tugs one way and personal preference another.

This book will help the pastor grow in his or her understanding of the work-life and the moral dilemmas of other persons in their own occupational worlds, professionals in particular. Theological ethicist James Gustafson has argued that one role of the pastor is that of "moral counselor."[3] By looking at himself or herself as a professional who must order the work of ministry according to moral valuation, the minister can better assist others to do the same in their own respective places of service.

One final and important word of introduction remains. Ministry ethics reflects the more sober side of a calling that has many lighthearted, joyful moments. Conrad Hyers, commenting on the comic vision, said that tragedy often fails to celebrate grace because of its "consuming interest in nobility, honor, and prestige. Heroism, superiority, being number one, saving face, national pride: these are tragic concerns. The comic vision counters by paying particular attention to ordinary people, and especially the weak, the meek and the lowly."[4]

Avoiding those preoccupations, writings in pastoral ethics nonetheless often propose sober guidelines that lay claim to us. It is not the role of ethics to celebrate the freedom so much as the discipline that sustains us. The burden being light, and the yoke easy, however, ministry is a place of happiness and well-being. Reasoned guidance about our role comes to us as a gift more than a grind. By it we are as often freed from confusion as burdened by an obligation.

Law is one dimension of God's grace. Another dimension, in both doctrine and the human experience that lies behind it, is forgiveness and the subsequent joy of reconciliation. I will not be so maudlin as to rehearse the grievous violations of ministry ethics of which I myself am guilty. Nonetheless I hope that my own experience can prevent this discussion from a brittle or judgmental sobriety that makes the ordained ministry appear to be something other than the richly satisfying calling that it usually is. We are not interested in prestige, superiority, or saving face for the clergy. We are concerned for ordinary people and for witness among them to the grace of God.

Notes

1. Janet F. Fishburn and Neill Q. Hamilton, "Seminary Education Tested by Praxis," *The Christian Century* 101 (February 1-8, 1984): 108-12.

2. Ibid.

3. James Gustafson, "The Minister as Moral Counselor," *Proceedings*, Association for Professional Education for Ministry (1982).

4. Conrad Hyers, "The Comic Vision in a Tragic World," *The Christian Century* 100 (April 20, 1983): 363-67.

1.

A FRAMEWORK FOR PASTORAL ETHICS

The call of every profession, and of every serious-minded Christian for that matter, involves a dilemma. We must try to reconcile the often dissonant claims of ultimate goals and proximate responsibilities. For the ordained minister the dilemma may present itself as follows: Do I serve Christ or the congregation? Am I serving Christ in the way I serve the congregation? Or am I not?

Only the naive think all this to be easily worked out. "To be the church's servant is the minister's vocation," writes theologian Robert Paul, "but that will sometimes mean speaking with an authority derived from a much higher source than that of the 'communal authority' [of the congregation] . . . . [A]t times it will cut across the 'communal authority' that a local congregation imagines it has . . . as the body that pays [the] salary."

Ordained ministers must be "first of all the servant[s] of Jesus Christ and . . . prepared to speak with the authority of the gospel delivered to us in Jesus Christ," says Paul.[1] But there, of course, is the rub. Sometimes "the authority of the gospel" will come into the human scene through the congregation's wishes, against the private opinion that the clergy have rationalized to be "Christ's word." Deciding which is which and when is ethical work.

15

We would ask nothing less of any professional than to resist toadying to a client when that client's wishes fly in the face of justice or health, or in the face of accountability to society at large. The doctor does not prescribe drugs because a patient or the addict requests them. We would ask the minister to "speak the truth in love," to speak with Christian integrity without truckling to the popular whims of congregation or culture. However, rules of accountability to the client or the patient, or the parishioner, even against the "better judgment" of the professional, complicate that easy kind of statement. It is here, for example, that there is a preeminent dilemma for the lawyer, working under a mandated norm of serving the client's will even at the expense of what might be considered countervailing ethical claims. It is also one form of ethical dilemma for the pastor.

Scholar Alan Goldman argues at just this point against the lawyers' requirement that the attorney be "zealous" in pursuit of the client's aims. Under this professional code, he says, attorneys stretch ordinary moral obligations out of shape. "Here we find that it is not the lawyer's place to forgo on moral grounds any legal objectives that [the] client seeks." Various and notorious tricks of courtroom strategy come to be morally justified and even required in this perspective. The lawyer "may do for his [sic] client what he could not morally do for himself, his friend, or even his wife or child [if the action involves violating rights of others for trivial interests of his family]."[2] Goldman urges reform.

May the minister, in the pursuit of professional responsibility, do what would not be acceptable in ordinary social intercourse? Is distorting the truth for the sake of the welfare of the church permissible? Should the minister wheedle and exploit the gullible in raising funds—again "for the cause of Christ"? May he or she plagiarize when there is not time—or talent, perhaps—for preparation on one's own?

In his own helpful language, Goldman argues that the lawyer should not see the task of advocacy to be so "highly differentiated" as this, differentiated, that is, from more work-a-day moral norms. What is not morally permissible normally should not suddenly, in a professional role, be permissible on behalf of one's client. The profession should not have or require that license. (On the other hand, the judicial role *is* highly differentiated, says Goldman. Even against his or her own private opinion and a reigning moral sensitivity, the judge should be strict in following the law so as not to contravene statutory process and the long-term popular will, as expressed in legislation.)

Is the ordained ministry "highly differentiated"? Is there anything the pastor does *as a professional* that he or she would not do as an ordinary, reflective Christian? (We will argue in succeeding chapters for the "low differentiation" of the ministerial task in this case.) The minister who thinks in the "highly differentiated" manner might gather in more funds "for Christ and his church" by all manner of means from the credulous and naive, rationalizing that this is part of the professional role. The "less differentiated" would say: If ordinary folk ought not to exploit their neighbors, then I should not. (One eminent TV evangelist accepted by mail, over several years, the entire half-million-dollar estate of a widow, who was then left dependent on her children. "I am your pastor," the mail would say, and you need to send more funds. Confronted, the preacher's attorneys argued there was nothing wrong in what had been done and nothing more they could do.)

Again, the preacher might rationalize plagiarism "for the sake of more inspirational sermons and a stronger pastoral image," whereas the layperson would be cautioned against the theft of another's material.

We would stress, then, as a balance to Robert Paul's emphasis cited above, that Christ also speaks through the congregation, quite possibly against the minister's "better judgment." Nonetheless, for the minister to abdicate the right to take issue with the parishioner's wish when an absolute value is clear, is to betray a trust. To do that is to become a mere technician, shirking the broader responsibilities of the professional. The congregation engages the pastor to help it open the Word in the midst of its life, to interpret vigorously the ultimate ends of Christian faith and mission.

Whether highly or moderately "differentiated," the material for professional ethics arises in the mix of specialized competence and training, and of social and institutional expectations that lay particular responsibilities on our shoulders in a given vocation. To complete a framework for clergy ethics, therefore, we look first at the "promises" made by the professional and then at the institutional arrangements that charge professionals with particular responsibilities.

PROMISE-MAKING

Accepting a professional role is unavoidably a promise-making act. Without knowing them personally, people visit attorneys, physicians, or ordained ministers with certain expectations of conscientiousness, commitment, and competence that would not pertain in meeting ordinary strangers on a city street. People have a right to such expectations. Some of those expectations are embodied in the codes of ethics of the professions. By announcing availability as a professional—"attorney at law," "M.D.," "pastor"—promises are made to the public.

These promises are the central norms of professional ethics. They are the point of departure for discussing all the varied dilemmas and complexities of deciding, in the face of one situation or another, what ought to be done. These promises also charge us with broader, proactive responsibilities, as we shall see. Different as the realities are, ideally the doctor is especially committed to communal health, the lawyer and judge to justice, the minister to the increase of faith.

What implicit promises has the ordained minister made to the public? What does the stranger, approaching the cleric, have a right to believe is already promised? Four things at least.

18

First, ordination is a promise of a person's participating in and—to some extent, at least—representing the universal church. Restless with the institution we may be. Under formal orders of obedience to ecclesiastical authority, we may or may not be, depending on our denomination's polity. But we do not speak and act, once ordained, simply as individuals. People expect, and have a right to expect, a word of pastoral assistance or religious clarification on behalf of the Christian community. Even from within the least connectional, nonhierarchical churches, we are professionally charged to be aware of the impact of our action. It affects the church's witness in the world.

Professional codes make much of collegial loyalty. Professionals are found even to resist truth-telling when it denigrates a professional peer. Such concern is more than a self-serving "conspiracy against the laity," to quote one of George Bernard Shaw's jibes about professionals. That element *is* present; however, the concern also reflects, albeit in an often distorted way, a loyalty to the value being served by the profession and a belief that the profession as a mutually supportive entity does serve that value, whether it be health, justice, faith, or whatever.

Second, to whatever extent a church and its ordained leadership claim to be a part of the wider Body of Christ, that church and its pastor make promises to the public about worship. The details of these promises, again, are variable according to tradition. The visitor will be treated kindly, with respect, not ridiculed. There is an implicit promise that the visitor will hear scripture read and, ordinarily, expounded. If communion is celebrated, even in an informal service, the visitor, unless intolerant or overscrupulous, will not be offended. The more liturgically and traditionally oriented visitor might even claim a "right," even as a stranger, to hear in that eucharist the words of Institution, and to sense the classic fourfold rhythm of "taking, giving thanks, breaking, and giving."

Many a person returning from an "experimental" service of worship, with its balloons or banjos, may be angry rather

19

than simply disappointed. The anger stems from a sense of a breach of contract, a broken, implied promise. This is not at all to say that innovation, experimentation, and creative self-expression are to be excluded from public worship. Quite the contrary. It is to provide insight into the anger and into a dimension of professional responsibility. Sensitive clergy and congregations will interpret and plan adventure-some liturgical form so as to minimize this sense of betrayal.

Third, ordination represents a promise of learning and competence that are to undergird the preaching and teaching ministry. We expect a nurse to know something of pharmacology, not blindly to carry out the possibly garbled orders of a hospital administrator or a supervising physician. We expect a lawyer to know much of the law and how to find out the rest. As a stranger, in approaching an ordained minister, I have a right to expect reasonably intelligent, competent pastoral conversation and teaching. In the present social and ecclesiastical environment, the person accepting ordination implicitly promises continued compe-tence and the study necessary for maintaining it.

Fourth—and this is the most difficult and admittedly arguable of the points—the ordained minister, not unlike every Christian, has a responsibility to reflect the compassion of Jesus Christ. That is to say, approaching the professional minister, a stranger has a right to anticipate at least a minimal receptive competence in pastoral care. There is no "Christian personality" that can be imposed on the clergy. But in some way, the role of the minister, just as that of the doctor, includes a promise of availability as part of a helping profession. In chapters 4 and 5, we shall discuss the ethics of pastoral care.

Anyone announcing to the world "I am a doctor," or "I am a lawyer," or "I am an ordained minister" makes promises by that very act. The professional "professes," makes commit-ments. In pastoral ethics we explore those implicit promises in the case of the ordained minister or priest. Pastors need to know, more clearly than they often do, the answer not only to the hard question, What am I in this instance to do? but also to the question, What have I promised?

ASPECTS OF PROFESSIONAL COMMITMENT

A simple grid based on elements that define *profession* proves useful at this point. Adapting from James Glasse[3] and others, we may list such elements as follows: A professional (1) is educated in a body of knowledge; (2) makes a commitment of service; (3) is part of a peer group that sets standards of practice; (4) is in an institutional matrix that claims allegiance; and (5) serves immediate goals in the name of certain ultimate values; which are (6) specific to that profession. These aspects of obligation are charted on pages 22-23 with several illustrations.

Using the grid, for example, we can see that the physician (1) studies and practices medicine. She or he (2) "professes" medicine and its goals, often in a specific ceremony using the Hippocratic or the Geneva Oath at the time the M.D. degree is awarded. (3) A state medical board and a medical association of peers regulate and monitor standards of practice. (4) Institutionally, the physician works in relation not only to a guild, but usually as well to a hospital. (5) The proximate goals are the healing of patients. (6) The ultimate value served is deigned to be "health." The questions of professional ethics for the doctor may be organized around claims and norms coming from the oath (loyalty to a patient), the goal of advancing professional knowledge, and the institutional connections, all evaluated against the overriding rubric of health.

The ordained minister learns theology, and steps into service in relation not only to a denomination and through it to the whole church, but also to peers in the ordained ministry. Entry into that colleagueship is celebrated as the ordinand pledges churchly participation and loyalty. All of this is clearly designated for the mission of Christ and the

PROFESSIONAL

Profession	Body of Knowledge	Commitment Professional entry
Physician	Medicine	Hippocratic or Geneva Oath
Lawyer	Law	Canon of Legal Ethics
Ordained Minister	"Divinity," Theology	Ordination vows
Business Manager	Management, "Business Administration"	
Teacher	Pedagogy	Certification

RELATIONSHIPS

Source of Standards	Institutional Matrix	Immediate Goals	Ultimate Value Served
A.M.A. State Medical Board	Hospital	Cure the symptom or disease	Health
A.B.A.	Court	Win the case	Justice
Church Court, Judicatory	Church, Denomination	Recruit the member, Build the congregation	Faith
	Corporation	Build profit, Strengthen company, Achieve "performance goals"	Economic well-being of society
	School	Build high test scores for class	Educational growth: Wisdom, Learning, Citizenship, Work skill

extension of Christian faith, by means of the proximate goals of pastoral care and the building up of the church.

The grid serves to alert a professional group to weaknesses in its moral structure. The open squares on the chart reveal that a business executive could not easily specify content for professional commitment or the source of managerial standards. As practiced, business goals may fall too far short of the "economic well-being of society" for this field of endeavor to qualify as professional work, in our understanding. Another vacant square on the grid may suggest that public-school teachers may need to further refine and designate their professional standards.

This chart clarifies three further aspects of professional ethics, although we must defer any extended discussion of them. First, a professional has certain expertise and accountabilities, but only in relation to the professional field. As citizens, physicians have a concern for foreign policy or public school education, but their professional competence makes them no experts in those fields. They can only speak with special concern and competence about the public health disasters of a nuclear exchange, or health education in the schools. Likewise, clergy are called to shed light on the moral and spiritual dimensions of public as well as personal policy, but these imperative prophetic concerns do not give them warranty *as clergy* to claim expertise in welfare economics or diplomatic strategy. Confusing the one obligation with the other opportunity, an opportunity that is conferred by the minister's public position, leads to no end of unnecessary anguish for the church.

Second, the tension between the final two columns on the grid must be highlighted. The physician, for example, may experience considerable ambivalence as to the justice of spending enormous sums of money for the health care of a few while large-scale public health needs go unmet. The pastor experiences a similar tension when an affluent suburban congregation spends money on itself that could easily be spent on staff to supplement the mission with low-income congregations of the inner city.

The same tension relates to method. In the name of a proximate goal—enlarging the congregation—any parson knows of chauvinistic emphases that will recruit members while eroding Christian faith. Kierkegaard wrote of the recruiter for a temperance organization who found that by serving beer and wine he could attract new members!

The good professional has a wider awareness and commitment than the proximate concerns that normally define the day's work. To use an old cliche, the "professional" stonemason knows that he is building a cathedral and not simply chipping rock. The professional is self-critical in light of the ultimate value of the vocation, and regularly raises uncomfortable questions. Does the present deployment of health-care resources or clergy resources serve health or faith best? Should clergy salaries be pooled? We're not simply earning a living in our niche; we're working at the cathedral.

Third, part of the source of interprofessional conflict is here depicted. While all are presumably concerned for the human good, each profession emphasizes one aspect of that good and may be a little deaf toward other concerns. The lawyer thinks an apparently dying patient's affairs should be put in order, the hospital chaplain wants to speak of matters of faith and stresses death with dignity, and the medical staff thinks of the ways heroic measures might yet save the life.

Ralph Potter outlines four elements of ethical decision making that underlie moral and ethical disagreements.[4] (1) Two persons may perceive the empirical facts differently and therefore disagree as to requisite decision or policy. (2) Different loyalties may guide them, Protestant or Catholic, German or French, Republican or Democrat. (3) They may follow two different styles of moral reasoning, one being more utilitarian in outlook, the other more rule-oriented. (4) And they may speak from different "quasi-theological" beliefs that guide their group loyalty and reasoning. (One may hold to the "personhood" of the first trimester fetus, the other not—something not decided by observation, reasoning, or even loyalty.)

Following up on our analysis of professional ethics, we might suggest that professionals can disagree with one another for a fifth reason in addition to Potter's four. They have different responsibilities, different "contracts" with the community.

ETHICS AND THE MORE EXCELLENT WAY

Reinhold Niebuhr called the injunctions of the gospels "impossible possibilities." It is true that for Christians, one answer to the ethical question, How much shall I keep and how much shall I give away? is the answer Jesus gave to the rich young ruler: Give all you have to the poor. (Zacchaeus, volunteering before the command, suggested half, and he was commended.)

There is inspiring nobility in a Mother Teresa and those who take the vow of poverty for themselves, just as there is in thoroughgoing pacifists who cling to their position in spite of the tough questions of police power and international order. However, it will be clear already that while making use of the perspectives represented by the Sermon on the Mount and the hard commands of Jesus, we have also accepted an "interim ethic" of our own. The dominion of God, while "already come," will not be fully realized until the eschaton. We do not use the impossible possibilities as legislated requirements of all people, or of all Christians or of ordained ministers. Just as the creating and incarnate God affirms such social orders as the family and the state in the fallen world, so do we accept the embodied church and its leadership by salaried pastors who do not give everything or even half to the poor. They live among other Christians as participants in the same social order with no special obligation to   When the dominion of God wholly comes, there may be no parish congregations, let alone altar guilds and church bazaars. There will surely be no need for Enlistment Sunday, and for codes of ethics. There will be no self-promotion, no plagiarism, no authoritarian pastors, no gossips.

Meanwhile, however, ethical frameworks will be needed, continuing to generate realistic, normative perspectives that are plausible for ordained pastors, even though honored in the breach all too often. That is our task in the pages ahead. At the same time, we shall honor and affirm those who voluntarily take up a life-style well "above" professional norms, such as poverty and selflessness and long-suffering like that of Jesus Christ himself.

Notes

1. Robert S. Paul, *Ministry* (Grand Rapids: Wm. B. Eerdmans Publishing Co., 1965), p. 43.

2. Alan H. Goldman, *The Moral Foundations of Professional Ethics* (Totowa, N.J.: Rowman and Littlefield, 1980), pp. 93, 95.

3. James D. Glasse, *Profession: Minister* (Nashville: Abingdon Press, 1968), pp. 35-56.

4. Ralph Potter, *War and Moral Discourse* (Atlanta: John Knox Press, 1969), pp. 23ff.

2

THE ETHICS OF PASTORAL LEADERSHIP

We turn now to the functional areas of ordained ministry. How does ethical reasoning assist us in our pastoral responsibilities?

An ethics of ordained ministry cannot begin with rules. Ministry ethics cannot be first and foremost a code of behavior. The ethics of ministry must begin with the questions of what the profession is about, what it is up to, and what kind of personal intention and competence are therefore appropriate to it.

For reasons that will emerge directly, our first ethical concern for ministry is the ethics of leadership. The purpose of the ministry derives from the purpose of the church. We have a number of options for understanding that purpose. Avery Dulles outlines several of them. Each perspective has historical precedent, and each implies something about the kind of structure and leadership the church should have. The church, says Dulles, may be thought of as primarily as institution, or as mystical communion, sacrament, herald, or servant.

We may also begin, as the preaching of Jesus does, with the kingdom, the dominion of God.[1] The church is called to serve that end, the divine mission in the world, directed toward and tested by God's reign and realm. The church itself, that is, cannot be the ultimate test of the work of the minister, even though the purpose of the ministry derives from the church. Both church and ministry must seek to be conformed to God's dominion. Lest that beg too many further questions, we may settle perhaps for the well-known expression from H. Richard Niebuhr, "The increase among [all people] of the love of God and neighbor."[2]

This statement itself, of course, invites elaboration. What is the nature of faith? What kind of human activity increases the love of God, and what qualifies as "love of God"? For that matter, what evokes and what qualifies as the love of neighbor? Is the church to feed the hungry, govern in the midst of political chaos, save up capital for research and development in underdeveloped areas of the world? All these also serve God's dominion. Neighbor-love begs many questions. Nevertheless, Niebuhr's definition will help establish theological perspective for pastoral ethics.

If the ordained ministry derives its definition from the church, then the minister (or the chaplain, or the judicatory executive, or the religious teacher, or whoever as the case may be) works to help the Christian community increase its faith, and its will and ability to love God and neighbor. Niebuhr elaborates on the meaning of love:

> By love we mean at least these attitudes and actions: rejoicing in the presence of the beloved, gratitude, reverence and loyalty toward him. Love is rejoicing over the existence of the beloved one; it is the desire that he be rather than not be; it is longing for his presence when he is absent. . . . Love is gratitude: It is thankfulness for the existence of the beloved. . . . Love is reverence: it keeps its distance even as it draws near . . . . Love is loyalty: it is the willingness to let the self be destroyed rather than that the other cease to be. . . . It is loyalty to the other's cause—to his loyalty.[3]

FAITHFUL INTEGRITY

Living out that kind of love toward God and our human family is the work of a lifetime. It is not accomplished in a day or in a momentary conversion. Faith, however, is the human condition that moves in this direction. The task of the church is to increase that faith in the world. The ordained minister is an auxiliary in that calling, educated and appointed by the processes of the church toward that end.

Understanding this, the responsible minister acknowledges an obligation in the first instance to strive after being a person of religious integrity, a person of faith and spiritual wisdom. The ethics of religious leadership involves practicing theology not as a technical science but as a reflection on the Christian tradition in dialogue with present-day human life so that the church may better fulfill its task. Ordained ministry therefore involves prayer and study, time intentionally directed to God, whose Spirit makes present to us the truth of scripture. It involves an intention in our interpersonal and institutional relations to listen for the God who is present in the mundane affairs of church and world, the God who takes up even a cross to be fully present in that world. This is the starting point for ministry, just as for the physician the starting point is an ethical stance centered on the things that make for health, or in the case of a lawyer, for the integrity of the legal system and the things that make for justice.

The ethics of ministry, therefore, involves a personal focus of attention. The ordained minister who allows centrifugal temptations and frenetic activism to crowd out the possibilities for reflection, patience, and caring is violating—we may extend the meanings this far—his or her professional norms. Even if the activism is in the name of moral reform and institutional growth, the one who finds it impossible in the midst of work so to practice ministry as to be sustained in faith and hope and love, violates more than good practice for mental and spiritual health. He or she violates the vows of ordination. The professional in any field (using "professional" in our moral sense), must steadily resist the temptation to let institutional loyalties and immediate goals obscure the ultimate goals of the calling.

31

LEADERSHIP WITHIN, NOT ABOVE

Both insecurity and professional *hubris* are to be found in some assertions about the ordained ministry. During the '60s, there arose an ecumenical concern for the theology of the laity, and it evoked considerable defensiveness. "A doctrine of the church that concentrates all ministry in the hands of the total fellowship, the people of God," wrote Robert S. Paul, "does not seem to leave much justification for the specific calling of an ordained clergy." The comment reflected both a personal malaise and the discomfort of others. Expressing doubts about the staying power of pastors, Paul wrote that, "If one can add to the financial enticement the glamour of imagining oneself to be a 'frontline' fighter for the Cross behind a solid executive desk, the result can be predicted with reasonable certainty."[4]

Professor Paul refers with approval to Anthony Hanson, who equates the relationship between the ordained ministry and the church with that of the Remnant to Israel. The ministry "is the church in its pioneering form."[5] Paul tries to insist that ordained ministry is not something different from the membership of the church itself, but the Remnant analogy negates his argument. It leaves the impression of good faith in the clergy and betrayal by all the rest.

Professor Paul's contention, and that of similar worriers about pastoral identity, betrays a flawed understanding of ministry. A consensus—among both Catholics and Protestants—now holds that the whole Body of Christ is an instrument of God's mission in the world. Christ's ministry belongs first to the church, not to its ordained leadership. It *is* our hope that "front-line" self-consciousness, both Sunday and weekday, will be present in the life of every self-aware Christian who is taking up the armor of God against the internal and external powers of darkness. The pastor's role? The church appoints them to help expedite the witness and mission of the whole *laos*.

A healthy theology of the laity demands some rethinking on the part of clergy. The change in no way diminishes the

32

need for theological and biblical expertise in leadership or for pastoral direction that is able to assist the congregation into being a supportive, healing, and redemptive community in the world. Indeed, the change probably asks more of the pastor, not less. As laypeople learn more theology or are more profoundly involved in the mission of Christ, whether in the congregation or in the world, the pastor-teacher in whom they find professional resources for a better exercise of their Christian identity will be challenged to increase in competence.

LEADERSHIP STYLE

In developing an ethics of leadership, we emphasize style rather than rules. Our stance should now be clear. The minister does not own a congregation, although one might infer the opposite from the way some pastors refer to "my church." Theologically stated, the congregation belongs to God for God's mission of reconciliation in the world. The congregation or an ecclesiastical authority beyond the congregation or both call the minister to help the congregation better serve that mission.

In leadership style, then, all the resources of theological insight and behavioral science that help the minister move the congregation forward in ways consistent with its mission are important. One such insight is recognizing that enthusiastic deference to religious authority is not the same thing as faith, either for the individual or for the congregation. "Not every one who says to me, 'Lord, Lord,' shall enter the kingdom of heaven" (Matt. 7:21). In Jonestown, with its ghastly mass suicide, there was overwhelming devotion and deference to religious authority—authority gone berserk and demonic!

Christian faith has within it a striking suspicion of authority and a matching egalitarian stress. "You are not to be called rabbi, for you have one teacher, and you are all brethren. And call no man your father on earth, for you have one Father, who is in heaven. Neither be called masters, for you have one master, the Christ. He who is greatest among you shall be your servant" (Matt. 23:8-11). Even Thomas Oden, who is so deeply concerned for authority in the church leader, admits this stress in Christian spirituality:[6] "There is an awesome equalitarian strain implicit in the mystery of Christ's presence in the sacraments."

In India, I once heard a seminarian describing the power a village healer had over his followers. The seminarian spoke enviously: "With authority like that, think what we could do to build up a church." The student was on the way to becoming a Christian pastor. A wise critic sat patiently through the report and then said, "A pastor has some of that mystique. The question is whether to exploit and increase it or try to dispel it. Perhaps you would be usurping the place of Christ in a man's life, to have that power."

The chief moral expectation of any professional is self-discipline enough not to selfishly exploit the power that is entrusted to him or her. Ministry ethics commands us to be most wary about the way we exercise leadership. In active ministry, we are repeatedly invited, urged, and tempted to take center stage. We are accustomed to push for our own way in congregational life, forgetting the true purpose of ministry, which is to enhance the congregation's corporate life in truly Godward faith and genuine neighbor-love.

In secular language, we oppose "authoritarian" leadership, favoring in its place a "democratic" style. The latter does not mean the end of *authoritative* leadership. Indeed, lengthy educational preparation and the institutional commissioning so dramatized by the ordination rite both stress the pastor's responsibility. Competence simply involves nurturing the whole people of God and eschewing authoritarian temptations. It entails at least the following elements.

(1) *Collaborative leadership.* Ordained ministry is membership on a team. We live in covenant in the church, a covenant with God and with one another. "If one member suffers, all suffer together" (I Cor. 12:26). We are members of one body. The "loner" pastor is a contradiction in terms. There are

occasions, because of the prophetic dimension in ministry, when the pastor will seem to be set over and against the congregation. More of that later. At this point our emphasis must fall on the collaborative work with the *laos*, the people of God.

One result of neglecting collaboration is factionalism. Some leaders attract loyalty to themselves instead of building loyalty to Christ. It was this kind of factionalism that the apostle Paul had to combat in Corinth. "One of you says, 'I belong to Paul,' or 'I belong to Apollos,' or 'I belong to Cephas' " (I Cor. 1:12). The partisans did not see beyond their leaders to Christ.

Another hazard for the "loner" pastor is isolation. The ministry is occasionally characterized as a lonely profession. Typical medium-sized and small parishes have but one ordained, theologically trained minister, so professional colleagueship is not realized within the primary workplace. Not only are clergy subject to psychological and structural forces making for "loner" self-concepts, but a selective recruitment bias in that direction may operate as well.

Professional associations are difficult to sustain among the clergy. We might suggest a number of reasons for this—the emphasis on the private "call," the style of seminary education, the economics of ministry. To whatever extent all this makes for a noncollaborative style among clergy, it is unfortunate. Clergy are leaders *within* the church, *among* the people of God. Fundamentally, the minister is part of a collective—the congregation and the wider church.

Most seminary education fails to adequately socialize us into such a viewpoint and self-understanding. A lone leader, the professor, is dictator in the classroom, determining subject matter and syllabus, and often even doing virtually all the talking. Academic grading systems emphasize individualistic competition rather than collaboration.

Let but one case in ministry ethics illustrate our concern for a non-loner style of leadership and the proper deference to the welfare of the congregation. Hector Russell is pastor in a church where he has served for twenty years. He is seventy-two. The church has stipulated no age for retiring. Things go on as usual. The pastor and his close friends are proud that he can carry on so well at his age. His sermons however have grown familiar. The congregation is sleepy. Hector does a good job of being a pastor to the elderly, though to few others.

Out of responsibility to the church and its possibilities for new and vigorous life, and out of Christian humility that knows our human propensity for self-deception, Hector should resign even though he still has the political power to continue. Were the entrepreneur our primary model in the ministry, were the church a private business, Hector could continue without any blame. He is still, after all, earning a living. But clergy do not launch or claim parishes as their private enterprises. They serve them. The reason again: Clergy are auxiliaries for Christ's mission through the church.

We probably expect too much, of course, in asking all this of Hector. It is the responsibility of peers in the ministry, of lay leaders, and of leadership from the church's denominational connection to help Hector decide on prompt retirement.

Rules help, as do structures. The bishop is intervening in Hector's case, representing a new source of political influence not subject to Hector's control. A rule about retirement age serves the same purpose, once placed in congregational bylaws and denominational books of order.

(2) *Contract.* Conceptualize this accountability in ministry ethics by reference to the professional's "contract" with the client. That the professional's contract is largely unwritten and implicit, dependent on common understandings of obligation, makes it no less important. The courts, for example, still take testimony and award damages on the basis of deviations from standard professional practice and the ethos of a professional group.

In one respect, the ministry contract is unique. While the doctor has individual patients who seek relief and cure, and while the lawyer has clients who ask counsel, the minister's primary contract is with the parish. The minister's "client" is the congregation. The sermon, for example, is more than a teacher's lecture that is given to edify individual students. The sermon is part of corporate worship, upbuilding the congregation.

Pastoral care takes place within a congregation, and its resources include not only the pastor's person-to-person contact but also Word, sacrament, and congregation. (This means that pastoral counseling, if apart from the life of a congregation, is necessarily ambiguous.)

Leadership by the pastor is a collective, enabling activity alongside that of the natural and designated leaders of the congregation. The minister who usurps the role of lay leaders violates this ethic in a pattern not unlike that of a physician who ignores data from the laboratory or the business manager who ignores decisions coming from the firm's board of directors. In theological terms, the congregation belongs neither to the pastor nor to the laity, of course. Together, pastor and congregation are pledged to seek out the will of Christ.

The professional grid in chapter 1 shows the minister to be less of an exception in this institutional connection than the above discussion would imply. The physician must work within the hospital, and medicine is increasingly a matter of teamwork. Attorneys work with the courts, and many, indeed, are employees of corporate business firms, a structuring of their work that brings them new problems of professional integrity.

(3) *A guideline.* This collaborative emphasis leads us to one of the most definite rules of ministry ethics. The welfare of the congregation takes precedence over the professional ambition of the minister. A medical analogy: Innovative, dramatic, but high-risk operations are to proceed only if medically indicated for the patient, and only with informed consent, not because a doctor seeks more prestige, or even a breakthrough in medical knowledge.

A corollary for a specific ministerial situation: Neither the interim pastor nor an associate minister ought to be a

37

candidate for the office of senior pastor when that pastorate falls open. The genesis of this rule lies in our concern for the welfare of the congregation, not in any animosity toward either the interim or the assistant and each one's family. The case: James Bodmer is the young assistant minister in a large congregation at Glenview Church. He was appointed three years before by a committee that included the pastor; the action was confirmed by the church council. Bodmer's responsibility included a heavy load in youth ministry, and he has come to be highly popular with the teenage group and their parents. Now, this sector of the congregation immediately proposes that he become pastor, since the senior pastor has announced plans for a move to another church the first of July.

James Bodmer sees plenty of advantage in staying at Glenview. He has some roots in the community now. The advancement in salary would help him pay off his seminary debts and start a family. He would like to introduce a number of his own ideas that had been tabled by the senior minister.

The problem: Older people in the congregation do not know Bodmer well. They do not think of him as their pastor or as mature enough to carry the heavy responsibilities of Glenview. He was selected and appointed by an educational group at the time he was brought onto the staff. The proposal from the youth and their parents begins to divide the congregation.

If a full-scale search is conducted and Bodmer loses out, a significant and strong group of families is going to be disgruntled. Quite probably, the congregation will be hurt, even split in two. If a full-scale search is not conducted, Glenview will not have adequate assurance of strong leadership.

Rules help. Had an understanding about this kind of eventuality been written into Bodmer's letter of call, as is often done, or into the discipline of Glenview's denomination, or had it been deeply etched into Bodmer's professional sensibility, the misunderstanding would not have arisen. Rules need not be absolute. Most readers can cite happy exceptions. Where *unanimity* prevails, in a church of congregational polity, the call could be issued to Bodmer in spite of strong precedent to the contrary. In other polities it will be someone else's "turn" to lead Glenview, and Bodmer will have expected all along to move in other directions. The professional life is not simple entrepreneurialism. We return to this issue in chapter 7.

(4) *Nonpartisan leadership.* Our emphasis on the congregation as "client" and on the congregation's welfare should not be taken to mean that the best reaction to controversy is always to squelch it. In a typical church fight, two temptations present themselves to the pastor, both to be avoided. One is to bend every effort toward suppressing the struggle, using the authority of ministry to that end. The other is to attempt, in the name of neutrality, to stand completely apart from the fray. Good leadership chooses another course. Controversy, for one thing, indicates life in a church, passionate concern about its affairs. Absolute equilibrium exists only in a state of death. In any living organism there is constant ebb and flow, tension and resolution. Controversy is therefore to be acknowledged and used for its educative and growth-making value, not repressed. Good leadership does not have to take sides to live with controversy creatively.

In one of the most widely used of all case studies in practical theology, a Reverend Mr. Anderson is pastor of Walnut Avenue Church.[7] The church's steeple has been hit by lightning, and the large rebuilding proposal provokes a split in the congregation. Not all want to restore the steeple. Some believe the money involved should be used in social mission to the community. Anderson stays aloof, preaching "reconciliation, brotherly love, and forgiveness." He misses the educative opportunities that are latent in the struggle, a vigorous interest that could be invested in study and debate on the purpose and mission of the church. Instead of resulting in either learning or fund raising, the people's energy simply heats up in destructive controversy with one another. Nonpartisan leadership does not equal apathetic isolation from the issues. In the interest of tougher faith and a more vigorous congregational life, it needs actively to teach about both the process of communal decision making and the issues.

AN ETHICS OF MANAGEMENT

The pastor is inevitably something of a manager for an institution. There is nothing in this that is unique to the ministry. The farmer now manages an "agribusiness," and the doctor, often enough, a "physician's corporation." Managerial issues in ethics therefore come into play—fair compensation and recognition, just termination procedures, good incentives, appropriate contracting and purchasing patterns, adherence to legal restraints such as fire codes, prudential insurance coverages, and the like.

The frustration many clergy experience in their managerial responsibilities comes in part from a failure to accept this aspect of the work as important. Much more central to ministry, they feel, are the encounters of pastoral care, teaching, liturgical leadership, and preaching. Yet, if the "client" is congregation, the nurture and "management" of the corporate life and mission of the parish are integral to our calling. At the same time, this understanding means that there can be no easy separating of the management task from pastoral ethics. The norms of pastoral concern for persons and for moral standards in doing the church's business will guide us. We cannot adopt a "management model" for ministry, if that expression implies that the business management focus on efficiency and profit-making is to be the dominant concern that shapes our work. We do evaluate our efforts, of course, and our use of time. But the managerial dimension in ministry must serve and not subvert the ultimate goal of faith.

We stress, therefore, the application of conscientious management ethics to church life. It is tempting, for example, for the pastor to exempt the church from moral restraints that should guide other business and institutional life. Church hospitals have been notorious in expecting employees to work for less than their peers in other institutions and still not to unionize and protest. Paid church custodians and secretaries are often forced to forgo benefits they would earn across the street. Lay leaders, themselves offering without charge many hours to the church's work, easily fall into the same but unfair assumptions about church employees. They and the pastor rationalize the injustice as a way of saving money for a good cause instead of acknowledging it for what it is: an unfair way of saving their own and their friends' money.

The Christian position rejects the purely utilitarian ethic that charges whatever the market will bear and pays only what is necessary, without moral compunction. Particularly in the church, we must look to the morality of our own managerial life. Just as the church should tutor family and social life by modeling a rich and caring communal existence of its own, the church needs to be an example of reflective, responsible business practice.

Again, the role of the minister as *collaborative* manager is not unique. While the stereotype of business leadership portrays a top-down exercise of power, the paycheck being the magic motivator of subordinates, managerial science knows business leadership must actually work with a keen awareness of human relations and interactive organizational systems. Management literature does not discount pay scales and benefits as motivators, but it invests many more pages on other factors that make for human initiative and job satisfaction.

In the management role, then, the good minister works *with* lay leaders. The minister becomes supervisor. Decision-maker some of the time, more often she or he defers to designated, responsible officials in the lay structure so as to build up the congregation. The minister does not usurp the prerogatives of governance merely for the sake of efficiency, or of getting his or her own way.

If the above guidelines about fair compensation apply

41

primarily to employed staff, they also relate to the occasion when we request professionals among the membership to do small jobs for the church. In a large church, for example, a relatively inactive member, a commercial artist, was asked by the associate minister to help design some publicity. The artist turned in a bill when the project was done. The charge came as an absolute surprise to the young associate. Nothing had been said about compensation. Many professionals give their work to the churches, and lay leaders and pastors should have no qualms about suggesting this kind of contribution, but let the terms be clear from the start. Some guidelines follow:

(1) *No pigeonholes for volunteers.* With all our professional emphasis on expertise, it is tempting to defer to the specialized secular competencies of laypeople as they are recruited into the church. A good accountant for example should make a good church treasurer. There is advantage, however, in recruiting on what might be called a "zero assumption" basis. In pursuing church work, a person may want desperately to pursue an activity quite different from his or her own occupation. A teacher of English may want to sing; a business executive may want to tend the shrubs.

Moreover, secular understandings may be inappropriately imported into the church. A church is neither a business nor a mental health agency nor a public school, even while having likeness to each. The professional from one of these fields may bring in unhelpful assumptions and put them to work.

Finally, the church should not depend on a well-educated elite at the expense of no participation by the untutored. Many who have very humble work assignments and status in the weekday world can often gain self-respect through exercising leadership within the church. Neighborhood organizations in one depressed, low-income urban district seemed repeatedly to be led by unusually able members that came from one minority church. Someone asked the pastor whether his congregation was not made up of an elite class rather than a cross section of the neighborhood. "Quite the contrary," he said. "We simply put all our humble folk to work and train them in leadership and public concern."

There is both an art and an obligation in the "care and feeding of volunteers." The minister should help the congregation show appreciation for their efforts. Moreover, well trained lay leaders can multiply the leadership efforts of the pastor many times over. Both a concern for efficiency, then, and a sound theology of the laity lead us toward the collaborative style.

(2) *Fairness.* The actual lines of authority in the supervision of church employees vary with denominational and local church bylaws. In one instance the pastor is virtually a chief executive officer, with authority in personnel matters. In another, lay leaders have supervisory responsibility over at least some of the church staff.

Whatever the organizational structure, fairness to staff requires clear job descriptions and personnel policies. Lines of reporting and procedures for annual review should be spelled out. Holiday and vacation arrangements should be defined when a person is taken onto staff, as well as provisions for terminating the position by either party. Careless or callous management of personnel relationships is not excused simply because a church is the employer.

One of the most irresponsible of the church's present-day practices has to do with female clergy. The important question, easy enough to formulate, is, Would a man have been treated the same way? In one church, a fully ordained professional woman was added to the staff as minister of education and youth. According to denominational policy, the church was obliged to provide housing. The parish had two parsonages for its other two staff clergy, both males. The young woman, not wanting to be pushy, accepted a small apartment rented for her by the congregation. When one of the male clergy left, however, and was not to be replaced, the young woman naturally assumed that one of the parsonages would become her residence. She was devastated by the church's decision to rent it out, with the rental covering her apartment expenses, and considerably more. If able to be honest with themselves, most of those on the church's administrative board would have admitted that a male, single or not, would have been given the house. Unfortunately, the remaining ordained male did not invest his teaching and administrative authority to urge a fairer decision.

Again, the church should be a bellwether and pioneer in affirmative action, hoping that the quality of its own administrative life can move other societal organizations toward justice.

(3) *Standard practices.* A range of administrative details need be but listed. Most of them can be managed by good lay leadership, but the ordained minister will keep them in mind because of his or her particular overall responsibility. In some denominations these tasks loom large. Records are to be kept, and accurately. (Membership rolls, like expense accounts, ought not be padded, necessary as tact and Christian sensitivity are in purging them.) Property should be well maintained. Liability and property insurance need to be regularly reviewed, particularly in seasons of inflation. A larger project for many congregations, providing for the handicapped access to church buildings, will soon be a standard obligation.

MEDIATING WITHIN THE *OIKUMENE*

Implicit in the professional person's "body of knowledge" and "institutional matrix" as charted in chapter 1 is a mediating role. Because of their training and institutional connections, professionals provide clients access to a wider world. The primary physician can lead a patient to specialists in clinics across the country. The professor introduces a student to a whole tradition of learning. The minister has the responsibility of showing the parishioner the world of faith and of showing the local congregation the universal church, the *oikumene*. In some denominations the local church is seen as a cell within a wider regional body and accountable to it. Given that self-concept for the congregation, the mediating role for the pastor is wholly natural. But even in those traditions that stress "local autonomy," the pastor is shirking ministerial duty if the parish is not regularly informed, through preaching and teaching, of the mind of the universal church.

As much as clergy complain about mail from headquarters, pastoral letters from bishops and councils and their various counterparts are not for the wastebasket. Every Christian, though free in conscience, is bound within the Body of Christ to take seriously what other Christians are moved to confess and share. In many cases, the pastor is an indispensable link in this communication among Christians. Even if conscience moves the minister to oppose a resolution or an episcopal directive, ministry ethics would urge that the debate go forward by the route of sharing, not burying, this communication from the wider church. Such missives come with varying degrees of pertinence and claim, of course. One's own denomination, we would judge, and one's own region, would have first claim, coming from the "nearest" neighbors. The wider ecumenical church, nevertheless, should have its hearing, the Third World "younger churches" not the least.

CREATIVE LEADERSHIP AND ETHICAL RESTRAINT

The thrust of this chapter may seem one-sided. The reader may argue, "I don't see the imperative and the inspiration for the dynamic kind of leadership that we all know the church needs."

In fact, the pastor has immense leadership opportunity within the restraints of responsibility to the congregation and to the ministry of the laity that we have outlined. Week in and week out, specialized theological training is brought to bear in biblical text and human life as the people gather for worship. Day in and day out this full-time parson-person teaches and counsels as no one else in the parish, from within his or her theological perspective. Inevitably the pastor's comments at meetings outweigh the comments of virtually any other single person. If leadership restraint for the sake of growth among the laity results in an uninformed Christianity and a missionless congregation, that result probably reflects a weakness in the theology and the leadership skills of the pastor-teacher rather than the ethical restraints on self-centered authoritarian rule.

The conscientious pastor knows that the "right" decision by a congregation may often be one that goes against what would be the minister's own free vote. The pastor exercises no veto in ordinary congregational decisions, in spite of possessing the *de facto* power to do so. But the deliberative process emerges from a corporate life of worship and study and action, in which tradition and worship, teaching and preaching have all had their formative role. Even in very quiet management that brings forth these events in a congregation's life, the minister has power enough and to spare, without dictatorial practice. An ethics of leadership, therefore, stresses collective, collaborative governance.

However, a further note must be added about the free conscience of the minister. The representative, in a democratic state, is not bound to vote the constituency. Such a mechanical use of the legislative role would make a mockery of all deliberative assemblies. It would leave them as mere counting houses that could be replaced by computers. It would eliminate the legislator's own moral contribution as an autonomous human being. More grievously from our point of view, it would surrender to utilitarian ethical reasoning, opening the way to the kind of nose-counting majority rule that overrides the fundamental rights of minorities.

The legislator—in our case, the pastor—has the obligation, when such rights are in danger of being violated, to vote against the constituency. The ordained minister has an education and a denominational structure that undergird clerical decisions of conscience. Both may on rare occasion lead a pastor to conceive an issue as *not* subject to the congregation's vote. Instead, the pastor may stand in the way of it, using all the authority available, from the provisions in denominational disciplines to the personal power accumulated from ministry. The ultimate prerogative is the outright refusal to be a part of a decision, made by resignation.

At times of tension, balancing professional leadership and a proper deference to other Christians makes the pastor's leadership and managerial role a fascinating, frustrating, and exciting mix. It is also a deeply satisfying responsibility in those other more peaceful times when congregation and minister pull steadily together.

Notes

1. Thomas Franklin Omeara, o.p., *Theology of Ministry* (New York: Paulist Press, 1983), pp. 26ff.

2. H. Richard Niebuhr, *The Purpose of the Church and Its Ministry* (New York: Harper & Brothers, 1956).

3. Ibid., p. 35.

4. Paul, *Ministry*, p. 32.

5. Ibid., p. 62.

6. Thomas C. Oden, *Pastoral Theology: Essentials of Ministry* (San Francisco: Harper & Row, Publishers, 1983), chs. 1–3.

7. The case is available from the Intercollegiate Case Clearing House, Soldiers Field, Boston, MA 02163. (Case number: 9-372-293.)

3.

THE ETHICS OF PREACHING
AND TEACHING

The implicit and explicit professional promise of the ordained minister is to "preach the word . . . in season and out of season" (II Tim. 4:2). It is a tragedy of our secularized time that many laypeople forget or fail to understand the promise and norm implicit in the preaching of the Word. They encourage pastors who violate this dimension of professional responsibility, who preach smooth words from one source and another with little or no root in the Word. It is an equal shame that the task of exposition is handled with such a lack of imagination by ministers wholly orthodox in their preaching "under the word" that parishioners often either doze through the sermon or stay home altogether. The Old Testament epics and the Jesus who "always spoke in parables" speak to us in a lively spirit. Faithful preaching should be lively as well.

All of that is about a general responsibility. What, more specifically, do we mean by an "ethic of preaching"? There *is* an ethic to scientific research. Data are not to be fudged. Honest scientific method is integral to the ends of science. The ultimate end is knowledge, not the scientist's notoriety or promotion in the research institution. (Either goal might conceivably be advanced by fudging on the data.) Strictures against doctored data in scientific research are severe. When such distortions are uncovered, researchers lose not only their reputations, they lose their jobs.

But preaching is nowhere as clearcut a task as scientific research in the laboratory. There are varieties of preaching, and varieties of preaching gifts. Preaching is always evolving. Consider but one possibility as we look toward the future. Carol Gilligan argues against another researcher (Lawrence Kohlberg) about the ways people think and the ways they mature in moral thinking. On the basis of her own research, she proposes that women tend to be more wholistic and less linear than men in their reasoning style and moral development. If that is so, we shall be seeing a marked change in the styles of preaching in our churches. And indeed, books on women in ministry do make this emphasis.[1]

Preaching is as much an art as a science. We can ask, therefore, whether there is an ethics to such arts as writing novels or painting pictures. Such a query brings out issues more subtle than that of falsified laboratory data.

Artists take liberties. Norman Mailer uses language well beyond that of the newspaper journalist when he reports on a political convention or a convict's execution. His prose is evocative; he editorializes to an extent that is unethical for journalists in news accounts. The painter or sculptor does not usually aim at photographic or three-dimensional copying of visual or material reality. Rather, a point is being made through distortion and abstraction.

What then can be the substance of an "ethics" of storytelling and of aesthetic expression? An ethics for an art form speaks of honesty in a way different from honesty on a scientific research report. This honesty has to do with the internal coherence of plot or composition, with congruence between result and the purpose of the art work, and with the artist's relation, through the form, to the recipients of the work.

A woman who was reviewing a book by a minister said simply, "This book is dishonest." The book did not tell falsehoods. How can a book or a poem or a sermon be dishonest if it does not tell falsehoods? The minister was chronicling his "liberation" from an older selfhood in response to what he described as a religious call, one that he compared in glowing terms to the call of Abraham. The personal transition involved a painful separation from his wife and children, a divorce. The reviewer said that only late in the book, after the "call," was there reference to a new woman who entered the man's life, a new relationship. In checking the dates and sequences in the story, the reviewer said, the reader discovers that this new relationship began during the earlier period so idealized with religious terms. Sermons, like the book, can be inconsistent and dishonest without telling lies.

Besides looking toward aesthetics, we may look in other directions. We may stress the teaching purpose of the sermon. Then the moral dimensions of pedagogy—or 'andragogy', as Malcolm Knowles puts it[2]—enter the discussion. We may reflect on the way the sermon, not to speak of the entire liturgical life of a congregation, is one part of pastoral leadership and guidance. Ethical guidelines of many sorts bear on professional pastoral care (see chapter 5).

We may consider preaching in terms of congruence with the life of the preacher. Theologically hazardous as that step is, because preaching inevitably points to qualities of life that are beyond the full grasp of every preacher just as they are beyond the grasp of every Christian, it is hardly irrelevant. Does he practice what he preaches? is the question from the pew. One ethicist cited the problem of inconsistency in the following way. He accused one doctor of "judging that health or prolonged life takes precedence over all other values when it comes to patients, but not acting on that value ordering in the conduct of his own affairs."[3] A chain-smoking physician would be a case in point.

A number of concerns come to light, then, when we look at preaching through the lens of professional ethics and responsibility. There is (1) the matter of faithfulness to the true goal of preaching. There is (2) the matter of accountability in relation to scripture. There is (3) the issue of integrity in the way we use sources, and in avoiding plagiarism. There is (4) the matter of respect for other participants in the preaching event—the congregation. And finally, (5) ethics suggests some affirmation and cautions in preaching on social issues.

FIDELITY IN PREACHING

If the faith of the whole church is to be increased, our preaching must point beyond the preaching itself. The substance of preaching is a pointing toward God—for the Christian, the God who is known in Jesus Christ. Because this is the goal, the point at which preaching is most likely to fail, ethically speaking, is through ego-centered distortion.

Our proximate concerns are real enough. We need to attract people to the church. (The widespread popularity of the preacher will help.) We need to claim the listener's attention. (Cleverness and good story-telling in the sermon will help.) We hope to persuade people. (We think of the arts of rhetoric and debate. We know something about emotional manipulation and expedient artifice.) We believe the sermon should communicate with authority. (One is pleased to hear that the sermon had "impact" and was especially memorable.) In any one of these concerns, however, the ultimate goal can be lost if the proximate goal takes center stage.

Elmer Gantry, who ended up a corrupt impostor of a parson, was born, said Sinclair Lewis, "to be a senator. He never said anything important, and he always said it sonorously. He could make 'Good morning' seem profound as Kant, welcoming as a brass band, and uplifting as a cathedral organ." You and I have met preachers who tried their good mornings that way. We have heard insubstantial sermons delivered that way.

It is awesomely easy for preachers to take themselves too seriously. Far better is a kind of delivery humble enough to match the limited content of the words. We need a prayerful modesty that in manner and intention joins the congregation in celebrating not the preacher or the preacher's prose but the Good News of God.

If the "art forms" or methods in preaching vary—narrative, reason, confession, exposition, argument, exhortation—three elements of substance seem perennial: proclamation, edification, and invitation.

(1) *Proclamation.* The word *preach* derives from a root that means "to proclaim publicly, to announce." In the English New Testament *preach* usually translates *evangelizo,* "to announce good news," or *kērussō,* "to proclaim, as a herald." Preaching that fails, over time, to rehearse explicitly and implicitly the truth and mercy of the God that Christians have learned to know through Christ—that preaching violates the professional norm for the Christian pastor.

(2) *Edification.* Why does faith require edification? As created beings into whom God breathes spirit, we are a combination of mind, will, and body, and we exercise all those capacities in our faith. Leaving any one of them aside truncates the believer's wholeness in faith. Christ taught as well as announced the realm and reign of God. To convey in Greek the whole meaning of the Shema's command to love God with heart, soul, and strength, the Gospel writers add Christ's words, "and with all your mind," when the Shema is cited (Mark 12:30 and par.). The pastor shares an ethical obligation with other teachers: the quest for and sharing of truth and knowledge. Many an ordination ritual includes the joint assignment, to be "pastor and teacher."

Let there be no hiding behind any professional cloaks, fostering obscurity for the sake of professional status. Pastors who leave their listeners unnecessarily ignorant of textual criticism in their preaching, for fear of complaints from the congregation, need to supplement the virtue of love with that of courage.

There is an understandable reaction against too much academic analysis of religion. Much of our teaching in the church, even of theology and Bible, has been sterile, secular, and unrelated to theology's goal of reflective understanding of God and of God's ways among us. Believers want to get on with their commitments in the faith. Analytic reflection is but one of the wide range of Godward religious activities and sensibilities. Others, for example, are awe, praise, joy, serenity, prophetic anger, and caring service. But faith, as one major strand in the long Christian tradition has it, seeks understanding. Faith seems, by whatever the laws of the religious life there are, to evolve not only compassion but also reasoned thoughtfulness as it expresses itself in the world. So there is an ethical responsibility to truth within the edifying or upbuilding responsibility of preaching.

(3) *Invitation*. Finally, preaching is invitational, like good teaching. *Evangelion*, the root for "evangelism," involves the assignment of inviting others into faith. "Winning others to the faith," with its prideful connotations, is an unfortunate modern idiom, for reasons that will become clearer as we consider the ethics of public relations and persuasion (chapter 9). But the pastor who fails to invite others into the way of faith by preaching and pastoral care is again failing to meet a professional norm. Certainly the sermon need not close with a formal invitation or an invitational hymn as it does in some traditions. We speak here of an element in the intent and ambience of preaching. Faith, as the old truism has it, is caught more than taught. Preaching should be such that faith may be caught from it, just as faith should be catchable from the experience of worship and congregational life. In virtually every congregation there are some who sit, figuratively speaking, "near the door," trying out the faith, hoping for it, inquiring, while relatively untutored in the lore of belief and Godward trust. We have a responsibility to the people near the door.

The invitational preacher knows that we do not force faith into a mind and heart and soul the way we drive a nail into a board or the way we pour water into a cup. The preacher "listens people into their own stories" in such a way that those stories are appropriated and evaluated in the light of the gospel story. As part of the invitation the preacher may articulate his or her own doubts and anguished puzzlements over the human predicament. This is a fully permissible path in preaching, for it brings to light the hunger and advent-waiting of the race.

Great preaching is more than an announcement, like one in the church bulletin or on a billboard, that Christ has come. It is creating an opening in our midst by means of putting Bible and human heart in dialogue with each other, suggesting then the possibilities of faith in God, so that God may enter that open space. Kierkegaard showed us that the gospel comes about through "indirect communication." Fred Craddock called the process "overhearing the Gospel."[4]

RESPONSIBILITY TO AND WITH SCRIPTURE

Integrity in preaching involves accountability to two claims on us, two that to some people seem to conflict with each other. We are called in the first instance to share the word of scripture much as we do the bread of communion. We break open the Word. And we are called to speak the truth; the canons of truth-telling also claim us. And this is the bind. In the post-Enlightenment world, with its concern—not to say its preoccupation—for historical fact and its Newtonian conception of reality, the thought-world in which many listeners dwell militates against an understanding of scripture.

Because the Bible speaks the language of another thought-world, because it speaks of miracles and demons and archangels, today's listener, if the preacher takes no account of this modern-day one-dimensional thought-world, can perceive the preaching as misrepresenting truth. A simple and serious rehearsal of the Bible's story is therefore not always enough. As always, the preaching task involves interpretation in relation to the thought-world of the listener. It involves translation. Many are the college sophomores who have backed away from religious faith because of being short-changed by preachers of their youth, preachers who failed to correct the naive literalist teaching of the earlier Sunday school years.

Martin Marty is fully justified in the way he presents an event of the 1950s. *Look* magazine, with cover publicity, carried an article claiming 150,000 "errors" in the New Testament. Some passages of course were reported as additions absent from the oldest manuscripts—the ending of Mark, or the story of the woman taken in adultery. Many people were upset. Among them were unsophisticated but thoughtful persons who reacted not against *Look* or against biblical scholarship, but against the clergy. Justifiably so, says Marty. "Why, they protested, did you not have the integrity to tell us years before about the unsettled character of the manuscripts? Why did you wait until public embarrassment forced you out into the open? What else are you holding back?" A higher standard of professional integrity in preaching and teaching would have avoided or considerably mitigated that kind of suspicion.[5]

Of course the motives of preachers who avoid a serious integration of these two loyalties—the one to Scripture and the other to clearly communicating truth in relation to a modern-day thought-world—are both honorable and less than honorable. The preacher may be too preoccupied with the more important aspects of the message to take account of who wrote what and when. On the other hand, the timid preacher may fear a fundamentalist stratum within the congregation. The more commonplace error results from a naive assumption that these matters are taken care of in the church school program, or that they do not matter.

Whatever the case, it is irresponsible to allow a modern congregation to believe that Genesis, for example, is meant and received by the central Christian tradition as a literal and factual account of paleontology or stone-age Middle Eastern history, or that the Gospels represent stenographic verbatim reporting on the words of the historical Jesus. Little is lost and much is gained by a deeper understanding of scripture and its development. The ethical preacher will share the learning of biblical scholarship. She or he will also share convictions and puzzlements, as one human being to another, without the sham of naive or literalist certainty about biblical texts that leaves so many laypeople confused, religiously illiterate, and feeling guilty because they can't reconcile their own well-educated doubts with the preacher's apparent believing. This kind of honesty will not pretend to justify and explain away all the violence of the Old Testament histories. Nor, to use a pet gripe of a friend of mine, will it exhort people to make Jesus the model for their lives when the preacher realizes that this simplistic exhortation is irrelevant to the particular life situations being discussed. Interpreting the "imitation of Christ" for present-day Christians, who are struggling with the crosscurrents of business, politics, or other morally stressful pursuits, demands sensitive exposition.

What about loyalty to the Word? The minister breaks the professional promise and the implicit covenant with the congregation by neglecting the text and tradition. Too many sermons become little more than a thought for the day out of current social commentary or self-help literature. The task, granted also the creative interpretation that we have cited above, is not easy. The apostle Paul, for example, shared Jesus' view that the world in its present form would not last a lifetime longer. "Loyalty to the Word" cannot require that we reconstruct a latter-day adventism. To disavow all the literalist use of apocalypticism is not to succumb to a fad. However, a sheer dismissal of all the Gospels' and Paul's emphasis on the imminence of God's action as altogether irrelevant and quaint is not a fulfillment of responsibility by the ordained pastor and teacher either. It may take a preacher years of struggle to be moderately satisfied with the preaching he or she does from these often difficult texts, but the enterprise is to be undertaken.

Although it cannot be called an ethical obligation, preachers now have a professional responsibility to give serious thought to preaching from the lectionary. There are several reasons for this. First, there is no better way to assure oneself of avoiding the solipsistic temptation to preach one's own favorite themes, use one's own favorite texts, and omit meanwhile great chunks of the best Christian and scriptural tradition. Second, holding oneself accountable for lectionary preaching serves the wider church in subtle ways. During a coffee break at the workplace, John Jones from Parish A meets Jack Jamison from Parish B, another Protestant congregation, or even a Catholic one. If the two discover they have on the Sunday before heard sermons treating the same texts, ecumenism is served. Third, the symbolism of adhering to the assigned texts, following scriptural listings that are available to the congregation, emphasizes the biblical grounding of the community of faith. We share a common life around a tradition far more meaty than the weekly reflections and topical selections of one man or woman in the pulpit. Finally, the spiritual rewards derived from a stronger consciousness of religious time, in this case the liturgical year, can be considerable.

Slavish adherence to a lectionary schedule for preaching is usually ill-advised when more pressing concerns of a congregation beg a direct address in preaching. There may have been a public tragedy with overwhelming emotional import on most members of the congregation, an intramural event like a church fire or a centennial, an urgent moral issue for the community's unavoidable reflection. But let these rare "topical" occasions bring us sermons too, with a text, rather than mere bits of advice, or a lecture, or an organizational exhortation.

One part of professional clergy responsibility is regularly to interweave scriptural images, lore, and allusions with current interpretations of faith and action. We may too easily assume biblical knowledge and sentiment on the part of parishioners and proceed with the matters at hand without rehearsing any of the biblical material. Or equally, as we realize the paucity of biblical understanding so often present, we may easily retreat into pastoral conversation based on current psychological fad, pop philosophy, and mere civic justification for public action. We speak of self-fulfillment without referring to the image of God in us. We argue for a civic-club level of community service without referring to the One who lays down his life for his friends, who takes up a cross, and whose mind we are urged by the apostle Paul to have in us. Or we speak of racial justice on the grounds of the Fourteenth Amendment without a comment on the profundity of a Galatians assertion that in Christ there is neither Jew nor Greek, slave nor free.

The responsibilities of ministry mean two things in respect to the Bible, therefore: faithfully and regularly steeping ourselves in Scripture, and a conscious, intelligent effort in preaching, pastoral work, and organizational leadership to ground the life of the community of faith in the lively word. Lacking that, ministry loses its identity and integrity too easily, and the community flounders. If professional ministry asks on occasion, Who are we and what are we good for in the post-modern world? let the definition be extended by this additional phrase: We are enablers and teachers in the community of faith, grounding our work and that community in *prayer* and in the *scriptures*.

INTEGRITY IN PREACHING

(1) *Plagiarism*. It is in failing to keep faith with truth that plagiarism is so wrong in preaching, even more than in the stealing of someone else's "property." One might argue, with consequentialist reasoning, that if more effective preaching results from using someone else's material, if faith is the more increased, then the imperative is to use it. The love of God, however, means also a love of truth. It is untruth to misrepresent others' material as one's own. Little harm and much good is done by citing sources, although we should do it inconspicuously, not as a name-dropping exercise of self-importance. Often, to avoid intrusive names and titles, one need only say, "Someone has written . . . ." A printed copy of the sermon, should it be distributed, may then carry a footnote.

Plagiarism, over time, deadens the creativity of the minister, so important in the life of the professional—as opposed to the "technician"—in the pulpit. "I would rather preach a poor sermon of my own than a good one from someone else," someone might say. That sentiment has to it the ring of integrity, much as we hope the poor sermon can be improved. And the long-term result is likely to be a better quality of congregational life. Plagiarism easily creates or heightens an incongruence between the pastor known in daily conversation and the pastor known in preaching. That lack of integrity weakens the personal ministries of the pastor.

Tradition puts liturgical prayer in a category different from preaching when it comes to plagiarism. People write books of prayers for the explicit purpose of use by others in worship, like set prayers from the tradition. Nonetheless, ministers within the tradition of free prayer and open liturgy may prefer to put into a church bulletin or to announce during worship the sources of prayers. Well-led worship does not lose its authenticity in such a procedure. Indeed, there is an educative value to the nonliturgical congregation as it learns that some of its prayer comes from the great tradition.

(2) *Copyright.* Perhaps even more commonplace than plagiarism in preaching is violating copyright in photocopying and in publicly broadcasting material that bears the tag "all rights reserved." For church groups, permissions are easily obtained. In the case of anthems for our choirs, we owe it to the composers and publishers—for the sake of a strong religious music publishing enterprise—to buy the copies we need. Intangible as these properties are, that is the law. We do not steal church candles and candlesticks from the manufacturers. Because it is so easy, do we now steal the rights of composers? Some judicatories of the church have been brought to court to show cause why they should not be prosecuted. In at least one case, the plaintiff has won the suit. Under current law, copyright for a new song lasts fifty years after the death of the composer. "Used with permission" should appear often on the duplicated copies of music in our churches, and should accompany extended quotations in teaching or study material.[6]

(3) *Slander and libel.* The journalist's ethic includes a strong

imperative, even while fully reporting information, not to libel. That ethic, of course, is reinforced by law. Beyond that, the journalist has even broader responsibility to the public and to the subjects of journalistic inquiry. Accuracy, lack of distortion and innuendo, as much objectivity as possible, the clear separation of editorializing from reporting—all these are part of the code. In recognition of the journalist's gifts to society, and in exchange for such accountabilities, the journalist is given certain protection. In spite of recent cases that have brought the principle into question, journalistic sources are protected. The journalist need not disclose them, if disclosure would possibly compromise or injure the source.

The pulpit does not carry with it any special protection from legal charges of slander or libel. In one recent case in the District of Columbia, a judge gave the owner of land next to a church an award of $60,000 because the church's pastor had called her an "old devil" and she had sued him for slander.[7]

Reporting inaccurate negative information in contexts other than preaching leaves open the way for similar suits. We are asked to write to an adoption agency, perhaps, about the competence of prospective adoptive parents, or to report to a social worker or a court on a family. Even if disclosure is authorized, this is not a protection for inaccurate information. It is wise to consult with the person making the authorization about anything that might be construed as inaccurate or negative, allowing for correction or even a withdrawal of the permission of disclosure. Gumper writes, "Allowing the subject of a negative report to view its contents in advance is particularly advisable where the report is a requirement for an application for a position and the authorization to disclose, accordingly, less than completely voluntary."[8]

The preacher is regularly tempted to use incidents and experiences from within the pastorate as material for sermons. Occasionally, a telephone call to secure permission for including a story will solve a problem. If sermons are published, or if any kind of offense may be taken, written permission should be secured. Radical modification of details is legitimate, so that even those involved in the situation are either oblivious to its reference or are so sure that no one else will identify them that they are not embarrassed. Usually it is best to avoid these illustrations altogether if they reflect in any negative way on present or former parishioners. History, fiction, Scripture, the current media, and a good imagination all together provide ample content for illustration and embellishment in preaching without resort to risky, firsthand stories.

FREEDOM OF THE PULPIT—AND PEW

The ordained preacher is accorded a unique freedom in Protestant tradition. "Freedom of the pulpit" is a byword, in spite of the fact that the congregation "employs" the speaker. The congregation does not control the interpretation and application of Scripture as presented by the expositor. The freedom is analogous to the liberty given the tenured teacher in the best traditions of academic freedom. A similar emphasis on strict autonomy is found in the other professions; the doctor, lawyer, accountant, or psychologist must not fudge data, in spite of the wishes of his or her corporate employer. This is one of the most basic meanings of *professional*.

The pastor and professor are trusted not to exploit the protected power afforded them in the professional's social contract. Of course each of these norms of free expression is violated often enough that steady vigilance and regular reiteration of the norm are essential. The disciplines of the professional guild will guide, but the whims of either the congregation or the political power of students and college trustees must not intrude. The norms support the goals of greater effectiveness in moral and spiritual leadership in the one case and free inquiry in the other.

Within these norms, the proper exercise of the given freedom is not always easy to determine. For example, a tenured university professor was accused of anti-Semitism because of a brief section in a course on racism. He identified one element in Zionism as racist. The question: Whose biases—those of the politicians, the Anti-Defamation League (which joined in the protest), or the professor—were most evident? Whose should carry the day? Personal bias is not supposed to color academic analysis, but a kind of bias inevitably plays some role in selecting the very area of one's research. The task—and this is a clue to the responsible exercise of freedom in the pulpit too—is to know the possible distortions that arise from bias and, as far as possible, to restrain them in responsibility to the task of learning and for the sake of truth.

At least three temptations beckon us toward misusing our free pulpits. Playing loose with factual data for the sake of argument or heightened drama is one. A preacher will say, "All the biblical writers insist . . ." when it is not true, or "Never before in human history" or "The greatest Christian leader of our time" when each is doubtful. Effective communication can do without the exaggeration, and truth will be served.

A second temptation is moral self-righteousness that condemns the sins of others without acknowledging the log in the eye of the beholder. Transnational corporations are excoriated, drunken drivers, adulterers, segregationists, rock 'n' roll fans, all who do not tithe, Marxist economists, Third World revolutionaries—all in a tone of voice that would imply the preacher and perhaps the whole congregation live altogether outside the influence of human sinfulness. There are better ways of presenting the law of God and the tragic distortions of human perception and intention that we call sin.

A third temptation is found in doctrinal self-righteousness. This is preaching that violates the ecumenical ethic that we shall discuss in chapter 7. It is preaching that apes the prayer of the Pharisee: I thank thee God that I am not like others. It testifies positively to its own doctrinal tradition, but then it goes on needlessly to berate the affirmations in belief

63

patterns of other religious traditions and Christian denominations. As more than one philosopher has put it, we may often be right in what we affirm, but we are more often wrong in what we deny. Such divisive chauvinistic preaching and teaching goes against the wholeness and unity of the wide and diverse body of Christ and the family of God. Let us testify, affirmatively, as the letter of John puts it, to what we have "heard . . . seen . . . . looked upon and touched" (I John 1:1) and leave it at that.

Christian preaching and teaching are not only invitational, they should also edify and build up. How often the testimony of a new believer is right in recounting the "blessings" or the affirmations that faith has brought, only then to go on to tear down that of someone else because it is not experienced or expressed in the same language or the same pattern of piety. The conscientious minister knows both rationally and intuitively that a "freedom of the pew" should match the freedom of the pulpit. Preaching and teaching by the church need to respect the human autonomy of the listener—inquirer and seasoned convert alike. Authentic faith does not result from fear or gullibility. It is freely chosen, freely lived into. Cornel West presents this side of pulpit freedom when he speaks of democracy as the result of Christianity, and proceeds to stress the accountability of the preacher to the laity:

> Democracy requires that accountability—of institutions to populace, of leaders to followers, of preachers to laity—be the center of any acceptable social vision. This accountability exists when people have control over the leaders and institutions that serve them. Democratic participation of people in the decision-making processes of institutions that regulate and govern their lives is a precondition for actualizing the Christian principle of the realization of human individuality in community.[9]

How can we say that the minister is given freedom and is also accountable to the congregation? An understanding of the professional "contract" helps at this point, as does restating the theology of ministry. The professional is given authoritarianism but for the sake of service. The minister promises to serve the congregation by assisting their growth in the faith. Tension and confrontation are part of growth. Good preaching invites both the believer and the inquirer to look toward the judging and redemptive Word. It may say, "The Word judges us." It may not say with its fundamental stance, "I judge you." (Rhetorically, of course, such a clause may appear.)

Theologically, the ministry of Christ is given to the church, not to a hierarchy. In ideal terms, the whole membership of the church, not preachers alone, are called to become a community of religious inquiry and growth, and a community of moral discourse and action. The pastor invites dialogue, therefore, and reflection, and disagreement. The minister educates and edifies rather than coerces in the preaching of the Word.

The moral need for this stance in leadership style has already been explained in the preceding chapter. One way of institutionalizing this freedom of the pew through allowances for lay initiative is suggested in chapter 8. As described there, conscientious "self-start social action groups" can be supported by a congregation even without full policy agreement by pastor and governing board.

PREACHING ON SOCIAL ISSUES

Good preaching cannot avoid touching on controversial issues of personal morality and social policy. Granted that fact, however, both pastoral concern and ministry ethics raise several questions for us. Is it cowardly to approach a clear-cut moral issue so gingerly as to allow some listeners to believe there are still two sides to the question? (There usually are.) Is it irresponsible to present but one side of an issue when a significant number of other Christians conscientiously hold to an opposite point of view? (Usually such a number do.) Is it a violation of implicit contract to "meddle in politics" in the sermon? Is it a violation of our charge to open God's word in the pulpit *not* so to "meddle"?

We have already pointed to the fundamental stance of preaching—interpreting the Word, inviting encounter with God. *Openness* is a crucial word at this point. Openness stands opposed to rigid dogmatism in preaching, whether of doctrine or application. The community is invited to grow in moral discourse and witness.

In his fine, small book *The Prophetic Imagination*,[10] Walter Brueggemann sees the prophets, Jesus of Nazareth among them, opening the way for faithful change by challenging the "royal consciousness" of encrusted traditionalism, deadened or rigid religious authoritarianism, and elitist political power. God's activity in the world must continually work for change against the tendency toward and the reality of such all-too-human a social situation. The prophets do not take on this burden as political leaders in civic administration or as revolutionaries. Theirs is the gift and burden of showing faithful and would-be faithful people the spiritually deadening nature of the status quo—"numbness" Brueggemann calls it. The poetic insight of the prophet helps people awake from the "royal consciousness" and strive toward communal shalom—peace, justice, social well-being.

The ethical burden of preaching can be summarized similarly. Pastoral authority in the pulpit does not carry with it the freedom to convert a sermon into a political speech of left or right or center. Sermons are not meant, in the first instance, to justify any social status quo—always under judgment from God as it is—or any retrenchment or any change. Sermons are meant to open to people the word, and that means helping them think and act in the world in response to God. Good preaching will regularly illustrate and clarify the gospel with allusions to both the personal and the social shape of people's lives and that of their culture, of course. The object, however, is worship and faithfulness to God.

The pastoral and the prophetic dimensions of ministry are

intimately linked, arguments to the contrary notwithstanding. The conscientious pastor cannot choose one and neglect the other. True pastoral caring knows human beings live in and derive moral meaning from their social environment. Concern for this environment is concern for persons. Moreover, true pastoral compassion cannot limit its shepherding concern to official members of the congregation. A sensitive prophetic attempt to help a congregation widen the horizons of its vision of service and witness is spiritual and pastoral action. Little religious growth will occur if false prophets preach only "peace, peace" when there is no peace. The new wine of deeper faith needs the new wineskins of penitent hearts, not benumbed, complacent ones.

IN SUM: THE PROMISE OF PREACHING

Protestant clergy find their most distinctive professional role as they preach. They are ministers of the Word.

Some definitions of preaching are narrower, of course, than others. But whatever the sermon's purpose—edification, evangelism, or even institutional exhortation related to the local "enlistment Sunday"—the sermon is expected to be an exposition of Christian truth for the benefit of the here-and-now congregation and of others who may listen in by air or read it in print. This is the promise. In our own way, in our own time, we are to "eat this scroll, and go, speak to the house of Israel" (Ezek. 3:1). As Oden says,[11] this approach to preaching responsibilities assumes a threefold correlation between "the revealed word in Christ, the written word of Scripture, and the proclaimed word in our own contemporary language." It also assumes a preacher whose spirit, by personal discipline and commitment, resonates to the Word.

That, of course, is an assumption of the most fantastic proportions, judging by sermons you and I have preached and heard. Yet, there it is, blaring forth an ethic for our responsibilities in preaching that both judges and guides us.

Once more we can thank the evangelist for including the text, "Who then can be saved? . . . . With God all things are possible" (Matt. 19:25-26). The way worship and the grace of God nourish and edify the church in spite of what is found in so many of our weak and mediocre sermons is itself proof of the miracle and mystery of the divine.

Notes

1. See e.g., Judith L. Weidman, ed., *Woman Ministers: How Women Are Re-defining Traditional Roles* (San Francisco: Harper & Row, Publishers, 1981).

2. See Knowles' *The Adult Learner* (Houston: Gulf Publishing Co., 1973).

3. Goldman, *Moral Foundations*, p. 19.

4. Fred B. Craddock, *Overhearing the Gospel* (Nashville: Abingdon, 1978).

5. Martin Marty, *The Public Church* (New York: Crossroad Books, 1981), p. 66.

6. See Lawton Posey, "All Rights Reserved," *The Christian Ministry*, January 1983.

7. Lindell L. Gumper, *Legal Issues in the Practice of Ministry* (Birmingham, Mich.: Psychological Studies and Consultation Program, 1981), pp. 21-22.

8. Ibid., p. 22.

9. Cornel West, *Prophesy Deliverance* (Philadelphia: Westminster Press, 1982), p. 18.

10. Walter Brueggemann, *The Prophetic Imagination* (Philadelphia: Fortress Press, 1978).

11. Oden, *Pastoral Theology*, p. 128.

4

ETHICAL CONCERNS IN PASTORAL CARE

The ordained minister's shepherding responsibilities raise up a host of ethical complexities. The pastor receives privileged information that may be important to the welfare of others; confidentiality becomes the issue. The minister has obligations to a religious tradition as well as to an individual parishioner's well-being; this makes for conflicting goals in offering counsel. Clergy have institutional responsibilities beyond personal pastoral care; sorting out the obligations demands an ethical framework. Such tensions come with the professional territory. This was symbolized in the professional grid in chapter 1.

A review of pastoral perspective must precede our discussing "applications" in chapter 5. If ethics is a matter of asking, What ought I to do? our concern is broader than a matter of rules, whether of confidentiality, contract, or accountability. What should I be up to as a Christian shepherd? In pastoral care, are we more like counselors or teachers or therapists or evangelists? How do these dimensions of our work coalesce?

THE MORAL SETTING FOR PASTORAL CARE

George Rimer, pastor, is visiting with a thirty-one-year-old social acquaintance, an investment consultant named Larry.

Larry is not a parishioner, but he has come to George because George married him to Patty four years earlier. Now Larry is experiencing difficulties in his marriage. He is contemplating divorce. He and Patty are pursuing separate careers. They have no children. They occasionally enjoy each other's company, but more often they quarrel. Each of them seems to enjoy other people more, people from within the workplace. Larry has an unmarried woman friend in brokerage who is particularly close. Neither Larry nor Patty goes much to church.

Larry talks with George about how Patty wants more freedom in the marriage. There has been some marriage counseling in the past—help in building relationships, household budgeting, sexual compatibility. In some desperation, because he doesn't yet feel sure about the divorce, Larry has turned to George.

George is well trained in counseling. Out of that background he wants Larry and Patty to do what is best for them, not simply something that satisfies anything George would prescribe as "right." Nonetheless, he is more and more convinced that if Larry and Patty divorce, they will simply take their problems with them. Not problems so much, he thinks, as shallowness. He wants to teach them about promises and selflessness and something about what is best for the human race, not just for them. He feels an obligation to raise theological questions with them. He believes that moral questions, the issues of marriage and divorce included, involve more than queries about what one feels like doing and what seems most beneficial for one private party or another. Yet George isn't sure whether, as a competent counselor, he has a right to introduce these convictions in his work with these two nonchurch persons.

Phyllis brings a dilemma fraught with pain. She shares with her pastor, Nancy Caruthers, the fact that Barry, her husband of ten years, has struck her for the second time, during a domestic quarrel. It is symptomatic of other strains in the marriage. Nancy, who herself has struggled for women's place in ministry and calls herself a feminist, confronts a counseling assignment at once simple and complex.

Violence is wrong; it's that simple. A covenant of marriage is ruptured with violence. Yet Nancy knows the relationship of husband and wife is intricately wrought. She stands ready to support Phyllis in separation and divorce, if Phyllis wants that, but she knows her own anger must not intrude. Or should it? There are so many factors to help Phyllis consider, factors Nancy hopes Phyllis will raise of her own accord: the need to act on her anger and not to continue allowing her own victimization; the dangers of religious rationalizations like "my cross" or "my punishment" that crop up in Phyllis's conversation; the importance of loyalty in marriage, even yet; the maintenance of the family unit, and its still constructive gifts to Brian and Sherry, Phyllis's and Barry's young children; the possibility—the Christian imperative?—of reconciliaton and forgiveness. A relationship is tragically flawed, but it is built of many cherished moments as well as suffering and pain. What, Nancy asks herself, is the meaning of helpful intervention in light of all that? "Hands off," she says to the pressures that arise from her own accumulated resentments. It is Phyllis's decision, Phyllis's unique marital relationship to evaluate. Nancy is midwife as the decision emerges.

In pastoral care and counseling the minister recognizes a relationship to the work of such other professionals as social case workers and psychotherapists. For pastoral ethics, there are pitfalls in that recognition as well as important advantages. Too simplistic a comparison of ministry with secular counseling results in a loss of pastoral perspective.

The relationship of priest and pastor to parishioner has always included a moral and didactic dimension. This is a dimension that is weakened or considerably disguised in the work of the analogous disciplines just mentioned.

Pastoral care long predated the modern counseling movement, as the histories of the shepherding work of priests and pastors testify.[1] The sacrament of penance evolved early in the history of the church. Over the centuries, various offices and procedures evolved for carrying out pastoral oversight.

Pastoral surveillance, however, has from time to time been insensitive and authoritarian enough—not to say brutal, as it was during the Inquisition and the Salem witch-burnings—that we may be tempted to reject even a hint that in pastoral care the minister should try to dictate another's personal moral life. Let pastoral care, we may say, play simply a sustaining, listening role, leaving the teaching to the pulpit, the classroom, or the study group.

If pastoral care is to be integrated with the whole work of the church in fostering faith, however, it will inevitably include the moral dimensions of personal well-being. Pastoral care has to be congruent with the preaching, worship, and education that are part of congregational life. George can remain "client-centered" and nonjudgmentally receptive in his time with Larry, but if he is a person of integrity, he will not abandon his deeper sensitivities to "the moral context of pastoral care."[2]

In the shepherding dimension of ministry, we have learned immensely from the counseling and psychotherapeutic disciplines. We have learned to stop moralizing, to listen at greater depth, to get out of the way, to see where our own hang-ups and peculiarities intrude and impede the healing process. To hold onto this learning is a fundamental ethical obligation. In the process of changing, however, pastoral care has come close to losing sight of the distinctive contribution it has to make on the human scene. For example, pastors should question the counseling goal represented by the phrase "psychological adjustment." That a person of faith be at least a little out of step with the world, a little unhappy with it, is inevitable in prophetic faith.

Again, for example, most church traditions hold to a seriousness in the making of marriage vows that is often absent from client-centered practice in psychotherapy. The pastor has a unique responsibility in counseling, one that goes beyond that of the social worker or other secular counselor. We have, as Don Browning suggests, a teaching, "rabbinic" role.[3] It would be irresponsible to hear out the person who is considering divorce, if that person has sought out a minister or *pastoral* counselor, and never to raise moral questions, questions that would not necessarily enter into the professional range of the psychotherapist. Helping the parishioner acknowledge his or her private goals of secularly viewed "self-fulfillment," while clearly a legitimate aspect of pastoral care, is simply not the whole of our task.

Paul Pruyser writes it another way. He fears that we often abdicate basic responsibilities that the persons coming to us are implicitly and properly asking us to assume. They select a pastor for counseling because of a hunch that the issues in their struggle somehow have to do with religious meaning and transcendent hopes. Pruyser suggests a number of religious "diagnostic variables" that are more appropriately the pastor's responsibility than those most commonly used by the psychologist.[4] While the psychologist may be concerned mainly with interpersonal relationships at work or in the family, for example, or with a variety of neuroses or personal problems, we have a responsibility to help the parishioner reflect also on his or her sense of hope, vocation, and providence—perspectives more related to faith than to psychology as a discipline.

The good pastoral counselor, of course, finds ways of using the insights of both psychotherapists and spiritual directors. We cannot draw hard and fast distinctions, but we may risk a guideline at this point. The pastor has a responsibility to relate to the parishioner and to conduct the counseling interview being conscious of God's presence within the situation. In pastoral counseling, God's ordering, forgiving, and redemptive presence to and within the human situation may or may not be made explicit. It is always at least implicit.

Once the pastor is free from being overly deferential to the secular disciplines, of course, the old danger arises again: the ethical issue of misusing power. In pastoral care it is the ever present temptation to exercise professional authority manipulatively. The first complaint against clergy in one study of patients and medical personnel was that of the clergy's "use of the hospital as an evangelistic field"[5] during their pastoral visits.

How do we misuse authority? For one thing, with a savior complex, we may try to solve problems that belong to others to solve for themselves. For another, we may want to make clones of counselees and parishioners. If the mathematics teacher can direct the student to learn the right way to solve the equations, why not teach the parishioner the "right" way to believe and behave? Obviously the analogy is false. Our stance in caring is open, receptive, and deeply affirming, even while we stand ready, in the pastoral conversation, to reflect, inform, and suggest as to moral perspective.

Beyond the humility required as a professional safeguard against wrongly exploiting pastoral authority, we need as deep a self-knowledge as possible for good pastoral care. This is the kind of self-knowledge gained in good clinical pastoral education. It is the kind gained through a continuing relationship in supervision such as that arranged by clergy groups who regularly bring their work to consultation sessions with sensitive therapists. Without such self-knowledge our own egoism easily diverts or distorts the moral and spiritual growth of the parishioner.

CONTRACT AND AVAILABILITY

Taking note of similarities between the minister's work and that of cognate professionals leads us toward several ethical concerns we have in common. One of these of course is the concept of "contract." It flows from the institutional matrix within which our work is set and from the promises we have made.

When a person undertakes the role of ordained minister within a congregation, it is understood that more than public and official roles like celebrating the sacraments, administering the parish organization, teaching, and preaching will be fulfilled. There is a more intimate, personal role. The person also becomes pastor—"shepherd" in the traditional metaphor. What contractual obligations are thus undertaken?

Both availability for counsel and freedom for pastoral initiative are implicit in the pastoral contract. Coming first in most ministers' priorities are the sick and the hospitalized, both because such persons are identifiable and accessible and because they are more likely than other people to be in need of pastoral assistance. The responsibility of the pastor is clearer at this point than at almost any

Ministry "contract" also suggests availability to members of the congregation for counsel. The minister who is away or unavailable many days of consecutive weeks violates this norm, particularly if no arrangements have been made with the congregation for a replacement. Information about making pastoral contact should be available through a secretary, answering machine, or family so that a pastor, a lay church leader, or a clergyperson designated to "cover" can return the call of the church member who is seeking counsel. Pastoral care need not be the chief skill or interest of a minister, but availability in crisis is a requirement.

Availability under the pastoral contract is a pitfall for the poorly organized minister. Lacking a schedule that assigns time to other aspects of pastoral and personal life, and possessing a love of people, she or he will find requests for compassionate counsel or perceived needs for visitation mushrooming into more than a full-time job in themselves. Other programmatic and missional dimensions of the work will suffer. Burnout comes to the compassionate, pastoral person as readily as it does to the compassionate social activist.

Better management of time and priority setting are not the only answers to this problem. The pastor may fail to appreciate and nurture the gifts and potential skills of lay caregivers. The laity are allies in the ministry of the church, not merely "clients," and as such they can assist the overburdened, disorganized pastor immensely.

WHO ARE IN THE "PARISH"?

Availability under the professional "contract" takes a peculiar twist for the minister. We have obligations beyond our membership, obligations that cannot be callously or casually dismissed. Traditionally, *parish* was a geographic term, a territory, as it is in the Louisiana "parishes" (counties) to this day, and as it is in much Roman Catholic usage. We stand reasonably available, therefore, to the unchurched of our area. The mission-oriented congregation knows that it engages the pastor on behalf of a wider community than the membership alone, just as it knows its own liturgical life is undertaken on behalf of the community. (This latter emphasis was a crucial point in Martin Thornton's perspective-building book, *Pastoral Theology*.[6] The difference between church folk and others, who may be in their own way profoundly moral and religious, is simply that the "outsiders" have not undertaken this missional service of prayer and witness through the church, for the world. It is theologically and spiritually corrupting to think about moral comparison between the two groups. The difference is vocational.)

The geographic concept of pastoral responsibility made sense historically because of religious establishment. One church system and its leadership were designated by the social order for religious oversight of the populace. The system was being eroded even before the Reformation, of course, and with the emphasis of "gathered" churches the old pattern was transformed in Western Europe and the New World. Today, with disestablishment, with many clergy and congregations sharing responsibility for the religious life of a community, and with people so mobile that typically they drive past ten other church buildings on the way to their own, the concept is workable only through ecumenical cooperation.

We have spoken of the unchurched. The matter of "being available" to members of other congregations in our pluralistic system, to others of either the same or different denominations, involves serious questions of pastoral ethics that are discussed in chapter 7.

One of the unique freedoms—and responsibilities—of the pastor can be expressed by the term *pastoral initiative*. It is characteristic of most other helping professionals that, as professionals, they do not seek out their clients. Nor does the culture afford them such access. A person would be suspicious of a psychotherapist or a lawyer who came to the door asking if services were needed. Barratry (inciting persons to litigation) has a bad name. But the pastor, by tradition, can reach out.

The limits to this responsibility are real. The funeral of the member is more urgent than that of the nonmember, following our accountability to the "nearer" neighbor. We do not proselytize members of other congregations, obviously. (Again, see chapter 7.) But when we are known socially to others, and where their ties to their own parish are so tenuous that they call on us rather than their own clergy, what then? If, as we have argued, ordained ministry does not freelance with individual clients but serves the congregation and the whole church, our guideline is obvious. In deference to strengthening the other congregation's witness we keep away. Again, close collegial ties help. There may be circumstances another pastor can explain that allow us to be of use in the situation.

The community's ministerium or its individual members or both must also share a broader responsibility for the "parish" area, for poverty, government corruption, poor education, under-financed public services, inadequate mental health care, a chemically and aesthetically polluted environment, and so forth. Such concerns should come to be shared by the congregations. Only the narrowest definitions of "faith" exclude interest in the public weal from the concerns of responsible religious leadership.

Are there other guidelines for "outsider" obligations? One, doubtless, is the religious education of unchurched children. Just as we consider it a right of a child to food and clothing, independent of the ability or willingness of the

79

parent, so too with our educational care of "outsider" children. If a child will come, or if parents will bring a child, we assume this responsibility. Making known our offer is part of the ethics of pastoral care.

Another broad responsibility is to the bereaved. Death levels us all, whether we are connected with the church or not, and bereavement is no time to quibble in judgment about who is adequately "Christian." Nor is this a time to exploit for the sake of making doctrinal points, as the church in former days did by refusing to bury persons who had committed suicide. We have an immense pastoral responsibility to such families. While pastoral action follows upon theological conviction, religious doctrine itself grew from pastoral and religious experience. Our current emphasis on *praxis* stands for the constant dialogue between experience and reflection. Our task is to heal, and to celebrate the compassionate love of God.

Weddings are a different matter. The justice of the peace can marry. Churches, and religious services led by their clergy, are not for sale. Other criteria must be weighed, besides the single desire of the outsider for a "nice church wedding." Many clergy simply limit their services to those couples in which one party, at least, holds local membership. In the matter of formerly divorced persons, there is great variety. Some clergy are prevented by their denominational books of order from conducting these weddings. That position makes a teaching point for all to hear, one about the sanctity of the marriage vow. It hardly solves all the pastoral dilemmas.

From the perspective of this chapter, clergy responsibility in deciding about marrying or not marrying involves at very least an assessment of intention. "Till death do us part" is the promise. This means that the divorced person, if the minister is available for such weddings at all, must give evidence of a sense of the gravity regarding the past failure in the wedding covenant. (Bishop John Spong reports favorably on a moving liturgical recognition of this failure, not a "blessing" of divorce so much as a grieving acknowledgment of it.[7] The service heightens the seriousness of the marriage vow rather than belittling it, and it opens the way for a community to be reconciled with the two persons now separated from each other.) Another dimension of the assessment made by most clergy has to do with religious faith. The pastor is acting not only to marry, but to marry in the presence of God, a mockery if the couple lack any sincere religious sensibilities. To say it again, the church and the pastor are not for hire. Further dimensions of wedding practice are discussed in chapters 6 and 7.

Pastoral availability to the geographic parish has to be severely limited in the time-consuming work of pastoral counseling. For members this availability is assumed. Most clergy will grant an initial interview for the "outsider" and move from there into a more extended relationship, or to referral.

REFERRAL

A 1950s landmark study of Americans and their mental health alerted clergy and other helping professionals to the poorly recognized role clergy play in mental health.[8] It also raised questions about our ability to make use of mental health colleagues for maximum assistance to parishioners. Few referrals were made, and there is evidence that far more were needed.

Referral is a matter for professional ethics because of our commitment to the well-being of the parishioner. Referral may be indicated, of course, for the simple reason that time needed for other dimensions of relationship in parish life will be taken by counseling. But the problem may be much more complex. If we cling to a relationship because of feelings of possessiveness or omnicompetence, or out of fear that our limited competence will be exposed to other professionals, then we violate our commitment. One young minister, unacquainted with psychiatric resources in his new community, and impressed with his own satisfying experiences in counseling at a previous parish, failed to note serious suicidal signs in a young parishioner during a pastoral interview. He failed even to schedule a follow-up appointment. The parishioner took his own life shortly thereafter.

There are compelling reasons that, as Ronald Lee puts it in a helpful article, referral needs to be seen as an "act of pastoral care." We have other obligations and cannot usually engage in long-term counseling where long-term care may be needed. We are not physicians, and pharmacological intervention may be of help to the parishioner. We are limited in our competence because we do not spend all our time in therapeutic work, and we are generally not trained in depth psychology. We are so accessible that many who would under other circumstances go directly to a psychiatrist or other therapist come to us as a port of entry. Self-knowledge and Christian humility should promote exploring and using referral in our pastoral care.

Resistance to referral provides a clue for self-knowledge for the pastor in the ways mentioned above. The parishioner's resistance can offer a step of insight for that person too. In discussing resistance to seeking help from someone other than the pastor, for example, a parishioner may come to a deeper understanding of internal ambivalence and conflict, matters that have been avoided in previous conversations that focused largely on external, problem. Nonetheless, we need to be alert to certain situational dynamics. Referral can be seen as a sign of rejection. The need for psychiatric help is still seen by many people as a sign of being bad or being "sick." It is important to note that referral need not mean terminating the one-on-one pastoral relationship altogether. Not only may regular congregational contacts continue—we may also choose what Lee calls a "relay" pattern, maintaining further appointments, much reduced in frequency and length, supportively "running alongside" while the baton is passed.

PROFESSIONAL DISTANCE

Effective pastoral ministry demands a nuanced balance of intimacy and professional distance. The right professional distance—a balance of empathy and objectivity—is a subtle concept for any conscientious helping professional. It is an especially difficult assignment for the pastor. We want to identify with people; we speak of unconditional love and caring; we strive for a deep rapport. But we must also remain separate enough from people's own profound inner turmoil that we can sustain objective judgment. Otherwise we can be of little help to them in their task of seeing ("knowing") into and through (*dia-gnosis*) their problems.

The professional should show enough coolheadedness to render fair judgment and intelligent service, without being swayed toward special favors or distorting excitements. Yet at the same time, he or she should be compassionate, warm, and caring toward the person or group being served. Within any helping relationship, the distance is part of what is helpful, a contribution of someone other than the very troubled self. But professional distance also contributes to the strength and autonomy of the client and parishioner. It helps avoid the ethical problems of paternalism and its correlative condition of dependency.

Professional distance does not mean indifference. It springs from affirming the parishioner's personal integrity and from an ethical commitment to truth and fairness within the community. By it we mean a disciplined approach to the helping process that prevents slipshod judgment and merely sentimental support. Through it, we also avoid potentially destructive sexual dynamics in the pastor-parishioner relationship.

THE MINISTER AS MORAL COUNSELOR

This chapter's perspective on the ethics of pastoral care portrays the minister, to use James Gustafson's phrase, as "moral counselor." Ethical reflection acknowledges the "oughtness" aspect of our daily existence, our moral vocation.

This approach to pastoral care ethics runs counter to much of what pastoral care appears to be about—the relief of anxiety and guilt. Moral counsel may appear to heighten both anxiety and a consciousness of guilt in a parishioner. It rests on an assumption that guilt can be and often is grounded in the objective situation, grounded in reality. It is not simply a feeling that needs to be removed like spilled milk. The twin assumption, of course, is equally important, that God forgives the penitent, and that Christian whole-ness—human wholeness—comes about in faith's acceptance of that gift from God.

Going beyond the comforting and sustaining role that is the substance of so much in our pastoral responsibilities is risky business. The holy is still awesome, even in our desacralized, disenchanted, modern world. People can shrink from God's justice, and all of us, in our own ways, shield our eyes from seeing God, "lest we die."

Five assumptions undergird this risk-taking approach to pastoral work, and it is urgent that we know them all.

(1) The goal of moral counseling, like that of other pastoral consultation, is insight and growth, not the expression of any conceivable moral superiority on the part of the counselor. The good pastor is profoundly aware of his or her own guilts and limitations, of life as a gift of God's grace, and of the constant need of God's mercy. Moral pride in the counselor is destructive. The pastor's own spiritual exercises must keep that destructive element to a minimum.

It is this taint of imperious and premature diagnosis that flaws Eduard Thurneysen's important book, *A Theology of Pastoral Care*,[9] as well as his lack of clinical reporting, so clearly pointed out by Edward Thornton. Thurneysen pushes toward what he calls the "breach" in the pastoral conversation, a moment when a parishioner breaks off human striving and prideful self-confidence because of a deep awareness of God's grace and the human need for it.

Thurneysen appears to believe this moment can be commanded by pastoral authority. At least in our culture, such a moment is more likely to come about by way of Christianly grounded empathy than from clerical preachment.

(2) Moral accountability emphasizes the personhood of a counselee-parishioner. It was Karl Menninger's plea in *Whatever Became of Sin?*[10] that we not denigrate people by turning them into mere pawns, victims of social pressures, without moral responsibility of their own.

We also acknowledge, of course, the collective pressures and deprivations in a person's life. It is for this reason that personal pastoral care is not to be offered without an awareness of the social and prophetic dimensions of ministry, an argument more fully expanded in chapter 8. Although stone walls do not a prison make, they do confine and shape a life. Consequently, caring ministry looks to the stone walls in this world, as well as to internal personal conflict.

The compromising executive, the cheating wife or husband, the exploitative landlord, the confused teenager who carries crib notes into an exam—all are enmeshed in a social system that pressures them toward violating personal moral responsibility, a system that exalts money making, shallow understandings of sexuality and interpersonal commitments, macho images of success. Moreover, moral issues are not all that clear to parishioners in the engulfing world of work. "Work hard but don't bust the rate," the tradesperson is told. "Charge what the market will bear but make it a fair price," hears the small entrepreneur. "Create the best transcript possible so you win an A-1 college admission, but never cheat," comes to the high-schooler. "Fulfill yourself at all cost, but be a faithful parent and spouse." In light of the confusing signals that bombard us all, the counselor's empathy is well warranted.

(3) Moral growth, as with insight in any pattern of therapy, must begin from where people are. To illustrate, let us consider the developmental scheme of Lawrence Kohlberg, useful for this purpose despite Carol Gilligan's critique

in other respects. Using empirical studies, Kohlberg describes six stages of reasoning about moral questions, steps through which children and adults seem to grow, more or less sequentially, as they mature. In "stage one" a child thinks only of avoiding punishment. In stage two, the child thinks a little more of reciprocity: If I do this, that person will do something for me. Stage three yields a larger consciousness of rules, and conventional morality begins. At stage four, there is an awareness of the need for morality so as to maintain the social order. Stage five moves to a clear effort at defining moral norms apart even from one's own narrower interest, norms arising from a sense of the social contract. A stage six person operates according to a self-chosen adherence to coherent, universal ethical principles. Kohlberg, who says that this framework is cross-cultural, reports that most adults don't grow much past stage four.

My purpose in referring to Kohlberg is simple. If Kohlberg is right, a leap to moral stage six is relatively implausible for someone at stage two or three. Preachments about the ideal can prevent our facilitating growth to stage four or five. Many ministers have failed to be helpful because of grandiose moralizing about the love of neighbor without taking into account the limited vision of their counselees and the situational constraints on them.

(4) The twin themes of moral law and God's mercy are the context for moral discussion. Without an intuition of the merciful promises, most people cannot even begin the often painful process of confessional insight and moral reflection.

(5) The method, like the goal, is still clarification and insight. We help parishioners to clarify the warrants and motives of their action, to define their root convictions, to see conflicting values, to explore both the emotional pressures and competing moral claims in the situation, and to evaluate consequences that follow possible courses of action. The decision is the parishioner's, not the pastor's. Pastoral care ethics sees the minister as moral counselor, but the moral counselor does not give out prescriptions.

As with other sectors of ministry ethics, we have approached the ethical questions of pastoral care by looking at the stance of ministry, at what the pastor is up to. Within the confines of theological conviction, church tradition, obligations of parish leadership, limited competence, the restraints of time, and the opportunities of being a "moral counselor," the pastor is a shepherd. Like Jesus himself, the minister often feels a community to be "harassed and helpless, like sheep without a shepherd" (Matt. 9:36). The burdens are not simply in the amount of caring needed. They also come in the ethical dilemmas shepherding presents. More specific applications of perspectives from this chapter follow in the next.

Notes

1. A number of books review parts of the history of pastoral care, among them, John T. McNeill, *A History of the Cure of Souls* (New York: Harper & Brothers, 1951); William R. Clebsch and Charles R. Jaekle, *Pastoral Care in Historical Perspective* (New York: Jason Aaronson, 1964); E. Brooks Holifield, *A History of Pastoral Care in America* (Nashville: Abingdon Press, 1983); Kenneth Leech, *Soul Friend* (San Francisco: Harper & Row, Publishers, 1980).

2. Don Browning, *The Moral Context of Pastoral Care* (Philadelphia: Westminster Press, 1976). See his first chapter.

3. Ibid., ch. 2.

4. Paul Pruyser, *The Minister as Diagnostician* (Philadelphia: Westminster Press, 1976), ch. 5.

5. Clyde C. Fry, "Ethics for Clergy in the Hospital Setting," (Report to the Academy of Parish Clergy, Annual Meeting, 1982), p. 2.

6. Martin Thornton, *Pastoral Theology: A Reorientation* (London: S.P.C.K., 1961).

7. John Shelby Spong, "Can the Church Bless Divorce?" *The Christian Century* 101 (November 28, 1984): 1126-27.

8. G. Gurin, J. Veroff, and S. Feld, *Americans View Their Mental Health* (New York: Basic Books, 1960).

9. Eduard Thurneysen, *A Theology of Pastoral Care* (Richmond: John Knox Press, 1962).

10. Karl Menninger, *Whatever Became of Sin?* (New York: Hawthorn Books, 1973).

5.

APPLICATIONS IN PASTORAL CARE

CONFIDENTIALITY

A fifteen-year-old tells her pastor that she and her boy-friend have slept together. She refers to her Catholic friends' description of making confession and says this is a secret, isn't it, between herself and the minister. It is not to be shared with her parents. Later, again in confidence, she tells the pastor she is pregnant.

Another teenager tells her seminarian youth leader that she keeps having thoughts of suicide, but that she has never talked it over with her parents, and is determined not to. She shares with the seminarian a death pact that she and one of her friends have drawn up. But no one else is to know.

To whom does information that is shared in confidence and confession with an ordained minister belong?

Few strengths for ministry are more important than the ability to keep confidences. Parishioners deeply need the freedom to trust this ability in their clergy if they are constructively to probe with pastoral help their moral and spiritual doubts, to confess their sins, and to grow. Confidentiality is enormously important, and wrenching ethical dilemmas arise when it seems justified or morally imperative to break it.

Confidentiality is constantly being eroded in our "information society." More and more information about more and more people is recorded in more and more data banks. Consider the traditionally private patient-doctor relationship. A medical journal reported that from twenty-five to one hundred doctors and administrators in a teaching hospital had the right and a legitimate need to examine a patient's records in a case of elective surgery, and that many others see the records too. Professionals in mental health and counseling centers routinely share clinical information with one another for the legitimate purposes of training and supervision, although the ordinary practice is to leave clients anonymous in these accountings. Group therapy replaces individual counseling. (One sociologist relates the introduction of the Roman Catholic liturgy's general confession, replacing the private confessional, to this trend.)

All this heightens the urgency for privacy somewhere, and the minister's study may be that place for many. The privacy of conversation with mentor and confessor and pastor remains a precious commodity, not to be squandered. The information "belongs" to the parishioner. One minister who spoke out of turn, indiscreetly imparting this kind of information, was sued for invasion of privacy.

One of our most difficult dilemmas arises from the multivalenced quality of the ministry contract. By adults, for example, the minister may be seen as teacher and steward of the traditional mores, *in loco parentis*. Yet the minister hopes to be an accessible friend and confessor and spiritual director of adolescents who are in transit toward a separate adulthood of their own, away from parents. Does this mean the pastor colludes with a fifteen-year-old girl in keeping her pregnancy secret from her parents, who are also parishioners?

Again, there are well-meaning parishioners, going about their own ministry, who ask the ordained leader to be their ally. Do we collude with a parishioner who asks that a spouse not be told of a malignancy? Does the minister favor husband or wife in a marital dispute, if one is more clearly at fault but both are pastoral charges? The minister "owes" something to each of two parties in every one of these situations. (In face of this particular dilemma, one of the most helpful conceptual tools for short-term conjoint marriage counseling is the pastor's attending to the relationship itself as "client," rather than to the two separate persons with all the other concerns and claims they bring.) For the pastor, the "client" cannot be made singular so easily as can the client for an attorney or a physician, even though analogous dilemmas often preoccupy these professionals as well.

We have not argued for a "highly differentiated" role for the clergy, warranting special privileges because of professional status, and special moral responsibilities not incumbent on other citizens. However, in the counseling role there is such a special responsibility. When something is learned in true pastoral conversation, what might ordinarily be shared with others is not shared.

At this point, we do not speak of mere gossip. Restraint on gossiping is incumbent on everyone. Rather we speak of a need to withhold even that information which might be constructive. Adding to a community's compassion toward those who suffer, for example, or simply strengthening the community through the mutual knowledge of members about one another, might seem worthy enough reasons to share what is learned through pastoral conversation. This church at large only with permission.

The reasons for this professional standard, of course, are backward-looking and forward-looking. In the past, personal stories have been shared in expectation that there will be no repeating of the information to others. In the future, with the pattern of confidentiality established and diligently maintained, parishioners will work with the pastor at greater depth in their efforts at soul searching.

William Harold Tiemann begins his helpful and singular book, *The Right to Silence*,[1] with a personal account. He had extensively counseled a couple whose marriage had ended in divorce, and whose children had been placed thereafter in a denominational children's home. Later, when one of the parents wanted custody, the home resisted in the belief that custody would not be in the best interests of the children. Tiemann was subpoenaed by the children's home as a witness in its behalf. What to do?

Tiemann did not testify. All his counseling, he argued, was privileged communication, protected by law. What he knew had been told him by parties who assumed that confidence would be kept; it was told him in the line of his official capacity as a clergyman.

In reviewing the tradition of privileged information, Tiemann's book reviews Roman Catholic canon law pertaining to the confessional. The problem for the Protestant pastor is more difficult. There is usually nothing so explicit as the stipulations and sanctions spelled out in Roman Catholic sacramental moment as Catholics have in formal private confession.

A LONG TRADITION

That pastoral conversation be confidential and not subject to forced disclosure is as important for the clergy as for psychiatrists and psychotherapists, and it is rooted for us in a much longer tradition. The helping process depends on an atmosphere of acceptance and trust, in which the client or parishioner feels free, without fear, for maximum self-disclosure. Tiemann recounts stories of those brave and knowledgeable ministers who, in spite of contempt citations, fines, and imprisonment, have refused to testify about parishioners or counselees. Their cases have usually been reversed on appeal, and both firmer judicial precedent and explicit statutory law, protecting the clergy's privileged conversations, have been the result. Usually such legislation reads in effect—and these laws are now on the books in most states—that the ordained minister "shall not be allowed or compelled" to disclose a confession or confidence incurred in the line of professional work. All ministerial codes strenuously emphasize the keeping of confidences as one of the most important of all their propositions. "I shall hold as sacred all confidences shared with me," states the minister's covenant of the American Baptist Churches in the U.S.A.

Confession to God and to priestly figures is virtually a universal aspect of religious practice. In our own Christian tradition, the seal on information disclosed in the confessional dates from the earliest years of the church's history. Leo I, the bishop of Rome in the mid–fifth century, ordered a stop to requirements of *public* confession and claimed apostolic precedent for his action.

> Although one must praise that plenitude of faith which, through fear of God does not shrink from blushing before men, yet since the sins of all those who seek penance are not of such a nature that they do not fear to have them published abroad, it is necessary to desist from [the public reading of confessions], lest many be put off from availing themselves of the remedies of penance.[2]

The Eastern Church was evidently more strict than the Western. A decree from the Second Synod of Dwin in A.D. 554 carried the warning: "A priest who reveals the confession of the penitents shall be deposed with anathema." Western manuals beginning in the ninth century are equally clear. Some add banishment to the penalty. One manual makes the "divulgence of a confession one of the four offenses so grave that for them no penance is possible."

In light of so strenuous a tradition, the notorious decision of a Nebraska prison chaplain a few years ago to report a prisoner who confessed to two murders during a counseling session appears, on the face of the account, to be highly questionable. "The chaplain said he feared that some inmates would no longer trust him after learning of the incident," said the account.[3] Quite so.

Nonetheless, some limits to an absolutist position on keeping confessional confidence are real, of course. Information about impending harm to the lives of others "belongs" to those others, although there is a legalistic confessional tradition to the contrary. Had the prisoner been revealing plans for another homicide upon an imminent release, counter arguments, defending the chaplain, would be appropriate. The minister, like others, is morally obligated to a concern for the safety of those he or she can protect. That moral claim, in this case, would override the importance of confidentiality. (Likewise, in this same case, one might argue for disclosure had another person been convicted for the murder confessed by the prisoner, and were persuasion toward a more public self-disclosure to seem futile.)

"Safety" introduces a very contemporary concern, as more and more child abuse comes to light. Those cases of child abuse discovered through simple observation by clergy or church school teachers ought to be followed up and reported to the proper authorities, as required of health personnel and educators. However, the laws in some states that require the ordained minister to report a child molester who seeks confidential pastoral help are another matter. If they withstand a constitutional test, which is doubtful, they should be repealed as too great an erosion of the confidential bond and too great an intrusion by the state into a religious realm. Unquestionably, the minister must insist that such a person seek clinical help immediately and withdraw from relationships in which the molesting is taking place. Pastoral care in this case means avoiding the cheap grace of forgiveness without both repentance and therapeutic remedy. The same is true of pastoral care for the batterer. But the freedom of privileged pastoral counsel is so important that legislation in this case is wrong. Moreover, it will probably have a negative effect. It would prevent parishioners and others from seeking religious help for fear of forced disclosure.

Such exceptions to a time-honored and sacrosanct tradition of privileged conversation conform to the professional's self-understanding. The professional holds responsibility for even larger social purposes than heroic adherence to carefully stated codes. He or she must occasionally exercise moral judgment that goes beyond the rulebook. The sometimes weighty task of taking on that kind of responsibility helps distinguish the professional from the technician.

Return now to the cases of the two teenagers at the opening of this chapter. In each of the cases, there are circumstances that might justify an exception to even so important a rule as confidentiality in pastoral counsel.

With the pregnant fifteen-year-old, there can be arguments on either side, but the first obligation, that of attempting to help the girl from a parish family toward disclosure to her parents either on her own or in supportive company with the pastor, is clear. Failing in this, only as a last resort, and if the parents are parishioners, I would argue for the right of these parents to participate in so urgent a matter for so young a person. Were she three years older, the pastor would be duty-bound to honor the privileged status of the confession. Were the teenager as well as her family otherwise quite unknown to the pastor, I would again defend strict confidence.

The seminarian case, with the apparently suicidal teen, presents a more clear-cut imperative for pastoral action, even in violation of the confidentiality norm. The situation involves potential harm (even death) to the child, even if by her own hand. That the seminarian (or a pastor, for that matter) is not a responsible clinical psychiatrist or therapist is to be assumed. The seminarian's supervisor is to be brought in, and the two of them will insist on an appointment with a mental health resource. This may amount to calling a bluff, but that step is at least educational for the parties involved. Like jokes about pistols in an airport's security queue, suicide talk is no trivial matter.

TELLING THE TRUTH WITH DYING PATIENTS

"Am I dying?" asks the patient, talking with the pastor. "Do I have long to live?" The family have kept up a cheerful front, avoiding talk of death. The physician has hoped to keep up the patient's spirits in spite of sharing with the family a conclusion that six months more would be "about all they could hope for." The family have shared that with the minister, and both they and the doctor draw the minister into the conspiracy of silence.

Both interprofessional relationships and pastoral ethics are at stake in the question of speaking truth with dying patients. For the minister, forthright disclosure of a bad prognosis when the doctor has withheld such information from the patient appears to violate a medical strategy that is in the domain of the physician. If the scene is set in the hospital, the pastor is already on medical turf, geographically. Guests do not violate a trust.

Nonetheless, the rightful claim of the patient, in putting a question to the pastor, would seem to override the interprofessional trust.[4] The patient is asking the minister out of an interest not so much in health of body as health of soul. The patient is moving out of the physician's turf. Sissela Bok, for one, along with hospital and hospice chaplains, argues that patients generally want the truth, even bad news, and that they are not usually depressed or harmed by it. It is fear of that harm that is used by doctors to justify what, in Goldman's language, is one more instance of "Hippocratic paternalism."

If there is anything that the pastor-parishioner relationship needs, for the sake of forwarding the spiritual maturity of both the parishioner and the congregation at large, it is an atmosphere of candor and 'integrity. Each of us could cite instances that tear at the fabric of trust. One occasion that eroded public trust, Bok remembers, was that of the U-2 incident in which lying was rationalized. To the American public President Eisenhower denied spy-plane flights over Russia only to be shown up as a liar because the pilot of such a plane was captured and in Russian hands. It "was intended as a routine lie to cover up for the reconnaissance mission of the pilot. It was for enemy consumption. But this lie was one of the crucial turning points in the spiraling loss of confidence by U.S. citizens in the word of their leaders."[5] Bok might have cited any number of similar deceptions, and far worse, about Vietnam, Watergate, and the Iran-Contra arms scandal.

"The damages associated with the disclosure of sad news or risks are rarer than physicians believe," says Bok, "and the benefits which result from being informed are more substantial, even measurably so. Pain is tolerated more easily, recovery from surgery is quicker, and cooperation with therapy is greatly improved."[6] Indeed, all this is to be expected, inasmuch as the patient is nonmanipulatively ascribed a human dignity that is wanting when that patient is being treated like a child. Counterfeit behavior by the family is replaced by a more natural sincerity. We argued earlier for the same kind of respect in urging on counselors a serious concern for the moral dimension of pastoral care.

Nonetheless, the pastor has no right to play doctor any more than to play God. It is altogether proper to reply to questions in situations of this sort, "You will have to ask your doctor about that," as long as the minister stands ready to be present with support when the doctor is forced to give a straightforward answer. One of the reasons physicians often avoid forthright prognosis is simply that there is limited ability to predict. Whatever the minister has heard from the family, or even from the doctor, there is probably more to be said in a heart-to-heart talk between patient and doctor. Inexplicable remissions do occur. Unexpected cures are effected. The minister cannot know all such statistical possibilities, nor, indeed, can every medical specialist. The discussion of these medical matters is not the business of the clergy. With only the rarest exceptions, keeping good faith with the medical team, especially on their hospital turf, is not only prudent but morally obligatory. That, too, can be explained to the patient.

Fortunately, with the rapid expansion of medical ethics discussions and our culture's recovery from treating death-talk as what Goeffrey Gorer once called a taboo-silenced "pornography," the amount of doctor-patient candor is rising. Medical ethics are stressing informed consent, and the maximum participation by the patient and the patient's family in medical decisions. (The patient, after all, *is* the employer of the medical counsel—the physician.) The dilemma alluded to above is less and less common. Moreover, doctors are increasingly willing to admit bewilderment, vague probabilities, varied possibilities. We want clergy to come out from behind professional false fronts, and so too the physician. There is no moral reason for a doctor not to share uncertainties; indeed, quite the opposite. The easy congruence of the doctor's twin goals—prolonging life and reducing suffering—no longer holds. The first may now increase the suffering almost indefinitely.

In more analytic terms, as was illustrated in our discussion of the chart in chapter 1, interprofessional tension arises from our differing foci of responsibility—health in the one case, faith in the other. Granted, *faith* is a nebulous and ambiguous term, but it does clearly involve for most of us a sense of self-conscious moral autonomy. In various instances, it involves an explicit knowledge that bodily safety and the mere prolonging of life are not the chiefest of all human values for the believer. In spite of the comment above about turf, when issues of this sort arise, the patient is walking through the minister's territory as much as that of the physician, and the pastor, even if physically in the medical environment, need not defer to the doctor.

Christians have claimed freedom to spend their health for good causes; to risk life in pursuit of noble ends; to defend kin and country; to accept martyrdom; to "lay down their lives for their friends." The "death with dignity" movement, with its "living wills" that limit heroic measures when the quality of life is irreversibly negligible and demeaning, comes from the same freedom.

CROSS GENDER PASTORAL CARE AND COUNSELING

Harry Downs has counseled Betty four times, each time realizing more and more the gifts of the woman as well as the loneliness and repressed pain she has experienced in her life. Betty is thirty-two, mother of two grade-school children, wife of Jack, a man on the way up in a construction firm. Her marriage, she says, seems to be going nowhere. As a child, Betty was very shy and fearful, and there are remnants of that in her yet. As a child also, Betty was sexually abused by an uncle, and she had told no one of these experiences until coming to trust the sensitive listening of Harry Downs. Betty has, Harry believes, too low an estimate of her own worth as a person and of her gifts as a worker or leader. He wants to affirm her in every way possible. They talk some about her going to work, now that the children are in school. Jack is hesitant, she says.

Betty is bright, and growing. She reads almost every book—theological or secular—that Harry happens to mention to her. Betty is more and more active in the church; Jack does not attend.

Each encounter has seen growth in Betty—less fearfulness and dependence, more outgoing exploration of new friendships and of new responsibilities in the church, outside the home. The counseling relationship has mellowed into a friendship, too. At the end of the fourth hour-long interview in about three months, in saying thank you, Betty holds out her cheek for a kiss. Harry finds himself gratified, and not a little disturbed. Suddenly he is thinking about whether Betty's relationship to him is the best thing for her own marriage and therefore for her, and for that matter, even for his own marriage.

There is no more frequent and painful a ministry-wrecking blunder than sexual involvement growing out of cross-gender pastoral care. A minister "falls in love" with a parishioner, and an affair or a divorce ensues. What also ensues is a crisis for a congregation, one that hampers its witness and mission.

Obviously, incidents of this kind are but symptoms of other elements in the situation. One cause of the problem can be an acquiescence to the romantic, cultural version of "love" that makes it less a matter of will and commitment and more one of being the victim of forces "bigger than both of us." Another may be a skewed value system that puts the self-centered search for personal happiness so far above caring for a spouse and family, integrity in ministry, and the welfare and mission of a congregation that new adventures supposedly favorable to such personal happiness are easily undertaken.

Cultural and psychological reflection that is more analytical may be cited. Janet Fishburn says that "clergy adultery is a sign of confusion about the professional role and status of ministers working in a 'marginal social institution.' "[7] Weaker male clergy seek manliness through successful managerial self-images, becoming ecclesiastical chief executive officers. Or they see themselves as influence-wielding change-agents in society. *Or* they compensate through sex outside marriage. Fishburn quotes the adulterous Tom Marshburn in John Updike's *A Month of Sundays*, who confesses he is a "poor WASP stung by the new work ethic of sufficient sex."

Certainly a minister's infidelities may in part be ascribed to a problem of personal insecurity, insecurity of such proportion that the pastor really is vulnerable to conscious or unconscious seduction by a parishioner. The situation may evolve from so weak a marriage in the manse (or parsonage) that a normally sensitive and caring parishioner actually creates the problem without an overt seductive intent at all. Or it may be that a shallow-minded lack of discretion in a lighthearted relationship simply leads on, with the support of one or more of these factors, to a full-blown affair.

There are two separate dimensions to our concern at this point. The more flagrant, by way of violating professional ethics, is sexual contact by clergy as they serve in pastoral care and counseling with a parishioner. The other, that of clergy divorce and adultery, also warrants comment.

Some general comments should precede discussion of the separate issues: (1) There is a sexual dimension to all cross-gender relationships. We cannot chop up the human person by categories; there is no absolute line of demarcation between spiritual, intellectual, and physical attraction in human relationship. Wholesome and hearty encounters like those in gregarious church activities, as well as those of a quieter and closer sort in counseling and pastoral care, draw subtle energy from the sexual dimension of cross-gender and, for that matter, same-sex rapport. Since we thank God for the joy of human friendship and happy group encounter, we can thank God for this simple fact of human sexuality. Being aware of this dimension of our human relationships is important so that we structure them well, because the power of more overt sexual involvements is potentially present. Sexuality is, like other gifts of the creation, ambiguous. It can be abused, just as it can be redemptively used. Therefore we order it in keeping with our commitments to the church's ministry, our promise-making in marriage, and our family responsibilities.

(2) We need to tend our own marriages and mental and spiritual health. In any field, it is often burnout of some sort that affects the professional who slips into alcoholism or adultery. The male minister who finds solace in the arms of a woman in the parish, with whom he needn't work on the daily complications of children's fevers, carrying out the garbage, or mowing the lawn—this minister is probably not getting on well at home. There is an art as well as a discipline to tending our marriages, and learning the art is one of the joys of a good marriage. There are suggestions related to this part of ministry ethics in chapter 10.

(3) We need to be deeply aware of human vulnerability— our own and that of parishioners. For ourselves, we needn't use the strong language of the demonic or take on repressive and puritanical postures simply to be reminded that temptation *is* around many of the corners in every life, that "the devil prowls" (I Pet. 5:8), and that ordered relations rather than sexual anarchy are part of the freedom for which Christ has set us free. Most of us cannot work happily apart from leisure-time companionship with good friends of both sexes. Building this kind of strength into our lives to

101

undergird our disciplines of religious commitment can help prevent some painful and tragic mistakes.

In our regard for parishioners, it is urgent to know that behind many pleasant faces there are anguish and loneliness, which may distort the pastoral relationship. The vulnerable parishioner can perceive personal affection and sexual innuendo that do not exist in the mind and intent of the minister. Here is a man, let us say, who in pulpit and chancel and general parish life is apparently always caring, gentle, and reliable. The parishioner knows her spouse is human and not always that way at all. In fact her husband may be sullen, brutish, or mean. Likewise, here is a woman in the ministry, always apparently pleasant, relaxed, attractive, gifted with the ability to look into the face of a man and speak significant things to his heart. The man has not met a woman like this before, and his wife, close-up and day-in-day-out, hardly measures up to such ideal virtue. The parishioner, whether twenty-five or sixty-five, easily reads too much into the pastoral caring of his or her minister. In counseling, encountering compassionate concern from this minister idol, the smallest gesture of affection may be misunderstood.

SEXUAL CONTACT WITH PARISHIONERS

I use at this point a helpful study-group report from an ecumenical body, the Washington (state) Association of Churches. The statement concludes that because of a conspiracy of silence around the matter, "Sexual abuse on the part of pastors and pastoral counselors . . . is more widespread than commonly believed."[8]

Even a little reflection makes the professional norms quite clear—or should. Parishioners in pastoral care are exceptionally vulnerable, and pastors, owing to their expertise, their status, and their symbolic role have considerable power. If they do not know themselves, of if they are charlatans, they can easily exploit a cross-gender relationship to their own advantage. The result, inevitably, is trauma to the parishioner and to the congregation. The committee report mentioned above is straightforward: "It is essential that the religious community understand the inadvisability and sin of a pastor or pastoral counselor . . . becoming romantically or sexually involved with a parishioner who comes to the pastor for counseling." The surprise, perhaps, is that the issues must be spelled out at all, since one might have thought that such knowledge and commitments could be assumed.

The report describes the difficulties comfronted by victims of such unethical practices, should they want to make complaints. Most parishioners don't know how to proceed, and many judicatories lack regular procedures anyway. This report urges judicatories to set up and to publicize committees to hear such complaints and to adjudicate. It also offers a list of guidelines for preventive, remedial, and reconciling steps, among them a firm removal of counselors and pastors from situations in which they might harm others similarly, until after repentance and therapy that bode well for future professional behavior.

One of the most salient statements of the report puts the matter solidly within the major perspective of this book: "When pastors of congregations are involved in these violations of professional ethics, the congregation is also a victim of the offense." Pastoral care of the congregation by the judicatory is strongly recommended, lest it be delayed in working through its own trauma and moving on with its mission.

Let there be some rules of thumb to serve as reflexes in the pastor and pastoral counselor. When cross-gender parishioner requests for pastoral help and time become unusually repetitive and persistent, look particularly at the probability of romantic transference. Likewise, a reciprocal willingness to provide that time and pastoral care should be an internal sign to the pastor. The issue is to be addressed openly. Referral should be arranged, if continued counseling is called for, unless the pastor is certain of the ability to be of continuing help without slipping deeper into a romantic attachment.

Given the vulnerability of the counselee or parishioner, and the variety of cultural norms, discretion should be exaggerated in pastoral care rather than relaxed. Even among sophisticated people who embrace in public gatherings, the restraints of a little greater formality are usually advisable in private counseling. Male pastors and female parishioners may have different expectations and definitions of "sexual contact." As the Washington report stated, " 'Sexual contact' is not limited to sexual intercourse."

Wherever possible, while adequate acoustic and visual privacy is to be maintained, cross-gender counseling should proceed in the proximity of other staff and parishioners. The scheduling of time and place for appointments needs to take this into account.

Lest the foregoing sound too severe, let it also be said that personal friendship within the parish is not against these rules. Janice is serving a middle-sized parish in her sixth year out of seminary, still single, but not committed to that status. Tom, an eligible male, in professional work, divorced, is a regular member of the parish. Janice has every right to a social life that is congruent with her increasing attraction to Tom. It can be seen as part of her teaching role, indeed, to be her naturally outgoing and vigorous self, and to resist any "third sex" ministerial stereotypes. She must realize, however, that pastoral counseling, should Tom need it, will be sought elsewhere.

The ethics of cross-gender sexual attraction and seduction may be extended with surprisingly little change to homosexual relationships. Homosexual advances by clergy toward parishioners of the same sex are just as wrong professionally. Usually, given our cultural homophobia, they seem even more scandalous to the innocent parishioner who is approached. Again, given the cultural situation, homosexual liaisons within or outside the parish open the ministry to obloquy even more serious than that directed at heterosexual affairs involving clergy, unfair as it may seem to the homosexual. As the mores evolve, faithful and permanent homosexual "marriages" for ordained clergy as for others may in time be another matter. As yet they are dysfunctional for pastoral ethics and parish leadership in nearly all but the congregations ministering to the homosexual community. Our teaching should help people mature in these matters. Nonetheless, we make a professional commitment to serve the congregation, a promise that may run counter to a number of our private "rights" and preferences.

CLERGY ADULTERY AND DIVORCE

We devote chapter 10 to questions of the pastor's personal life and to the matter of separating professional accountabilities from the private sphere. Professional identity in general—and doubtless this is even more the case for the pastor than for the doctor and the lawyer—is characterized by a blurring of the boundaries between the work-world and the private world.

There is no need at this point to discuss psychological or cultural sources of clergy adultery or divorce. Marriages do fail, among clergy as among others. Occasionally, without doubt, divorce is the lesser of two evils. Nor is the concern here in any way to suggest that when divorce does occur, the congregation should not work with the situation as redemptively as it is able. If it does not work redemptively, the investment of training and passion in a person's ministry may be lost. There has been a virtual quantum leap of theological understanding in many a congregation through the discovery that the pastor and the pastor's family are also fallibly human, subject to marital failure, even to the point of divorce. Nor should one read here a judgment on those who enter ministry after divorce, as an impressive number of competent men and women have done in recent years.

Our concern is for guidelines that may help prevent what are seen by many ministers themselves, after the fact, to be tragic missteps. I speak at this point primarily of males in ministry, not women. At present, for the most part, the problems appear to be different for women. The woman pastor needs to help men stop "protecting" her, an approach by male parishioners that demeans her professional competence and self-reliance. Most of the women in ministry at present have fought against enough odds that they appear to be less vulnerable than men to outside attractions or affairs that lead to divorce. Or they simply tread more carefully and flout community standards less easily.

These, then, are important guidelines: (1) The pastor is committed to teach and to follow a view that marriage vows are monogamous and lifelong. That is a church and a religious norm. We can be quite explicit about marital failure as *failure,* no matter how casual the culture may come to be about "serial polygamy." In spite of all the marital anguish and unfaithfulness, and the broken marriages of a typical congregation, this is an ideal those same congregations do want to uphold, just as veracity, violated on every side, is still the norm for Christian life.

(2) The pastoral couple should work especially hard at making a success of marriage and family life. This is not because they are supposed to be more virtuous than other Christians; all Christians are equally called to moral life. It is because the wholesome life of the "client" of this professional—the congregation—is terribly damaged by adulterous activity or by divorce on the part of the pastor.

(3) When the pastor finds himself or herself drawn toward an affair, counseling and spiritual direction should be sought promptly. If the marriage fails, or another seems so essential to the well-being of the parties involved as to overrule all the major requirements of the congregation and the maintenance of integrity in Christian leadership, then I believe good ministry ethics would generally recommend departing the community so as to minimize damage to local parish life. The parish may take initiative to the contrary, but the responsible pastor will plan to move.

SERVING AS REFERENCE

Jonathan Fairchild is a brilliant, sophisticated, and troubled ordained minister, subject to recurrent, incapacitating periods of depression. He has a supportive and forgiving wife who has lived through two episodes of Jonathan's depression and resulting infidelity. Denominational executives, out of respect for the man's gifts and out of loyalty to a colleague in ministry, and knowing of Fairchild's great potential for ministry, include his dossier and recommend him, among others, to a local congregation's search committee. They say nothing of Fairchild's previous problems, and they speak positively of his gifts. Fairchild is called.

Within six months the congregation has to give Jonathan a leave for convalescence during a depression, and within three years they are faced with clergy adultery, an affair between the minister and a parishioner-divorcee, a situation having a devastating effect on many individuals close to the pastor and on the congregation as a whole. Should the denominational leadership have acted differently? Was the problem to be attributed rather to a weak and careless search committee?

A minister must often consider how to respond to requests for recommendation. Character reference is often sought by a parishioner to be given in a court of law, or to a prospective employer or college admissions officer. Exaggerated comment that forwards the fortunes of the parishioner is tempting. Isn't it after all only a part of responsible pastoral care? There are personal advantages in what may even be rationalized as a "white" lie: What harm can it do? Negative, critical comments now risk exposure because so many files are available under right-to-know regulation.

The problem of "white" lies in this area is that they are not easily limited to inconsequential matters. The well-meaning pastor, whose letters exaggerate virtue to the point of lying, overlooks two aspects of the situation. First, the ones inquiring after letters of recommendation would like to hear the truth. Do they have a right to it? Presumably the one giving the pastor's name as a reference has reason to expect integrity of the pastor. Presumably, the clergyperson has a similar hope for truthful responses in a search for church personnel—organists, sextons, teachers, associate ministers. The minister has no such right, certainly, for truthfulness in return if he or she does not offer the truth.

Second, as is the case with medical placebos or clever manipulating of fact by lawyers, politicians, and accountants, even small misrepresentations erode the reliability of the profession at large. Hardly any distorting of the truth can be called wholly innocuous. As we see constantly in the advertising world, the coin of mutual trust is cheapened, and the rich network of human community is weakened. This is the kind of consequence so often overlooked by the utilitarian in piecing together a consequentialist "situation ethic"; not all the consequences are really taken into account. For reasons such as these, Augustine and Kant took a rigid stance on lying, arguing that it was always forbidden, even for the purpose of saving a life.[9] We cannot go so far. We more generally believe, for example, that if Anne Frank is hidden from the Nazis in a garret, we owe the inquiring police officer deception, not the facts. Lying and truth-telling cannot in so brittle a fashion be disjoined from other obligations to the good.

Nonetheless, let us all attempt our little contributions to the integrity of ministry communication. References should stay within the truth. We have moral obligations not only to our friends, parishioners, and colleagues, but to the recipient who is seeking the reference as well, be it congregation, admissions officer, or prospective employer. I discuss references for clergy in chapter 7.

INDEPENDENT PASTORAL COUNSELING

Obviously, we have proceeded on the assumption not only that the congregation is the normal recipient of pastoral care by the pastor, but also that the gifts of such ministry are best expressed in that setting. What then are we to make of the increasing number of more or less independent pastoral counselors and pastoral counseling centers, and what professional obligations have these counselors, if they have theological and ecclesiastical legitimacy at all?

It is, as they say, a free country. That the church (like the state) has an interest in what an individual does in hanging out a shingle advertising the availability of "pastoral counseling" arises not from a copyright on the word "pastoral" but from concern for protecting the public. There are too many inadequately prepared persons who, with this label, advertise their services and collect their fees; most states do not regulate this particular professional activity.

Many are those who want to help people by means of counseling while working from a religious world view rather than a secular one. They know that counseling techniques and one's belief system about human beings and human values cannot be neatly separated. They seek a career in pastoral counseling rather than secular psychotherapy, and rather than parish ministry. We wish them well.

At the same time, we must take with utmost seriousness the views of those who argue that independent pastoral counseling is virtually a contradiction in terms. Therefore, by far the most acceptable structure for pastoral care and counseling by those other than the pastors of congregations is under the auspices of a congregation or consortium of congregations. The sponsor should be clear to clients of the pastoral counseling center. Religious faith in the Judeo-Christian tradition is a corporate and communal reality, binding people into mutual care. Representing that corporate nature of religious faith with integrity, as well as drawing on the communal resources of church and synagogue life, is incumbent upon the pastoral counselor with anything more than shallow religious and theological understanding.

A second salient emphasis follows from our concerns for pastoral ethics. A pastoral counseling center engages in human service, not in profit taking. It must have a graded fee schedule and, if possible, salaried personnel, with openings for the destitute as well as the affluent. Like the church, it must strive to express the openness of God's mercy by saying whoever will may come.

Finally, the counselors who are pastoral will be professionally linked themselves with the church. They will be theologically educated and biblically aware, as well as versed in the caring and psychotherapeutic arts. They will be under the vows of ordination or, if unordained, will hold themselves similarly accountable to the life and mission of the church. On the other hand, by virtue of their calling, they will offer back into the more typical mainstream life of congregations their insights and experience. They will maintain an active colleagueship and dialogue with parish pastors and church judicatories. Similar colleagueship, and for many of the same reasons, is incumbent on those in other specialized ministries, such as hospital chaplains and campus ministers. They too have news from the front to bring to the home base of the church, and they too must see their work as an extension of the church, even as they are strained, from time to time, by (loyal) opposition to it.

If it operates within such a boundary, a pastoral counseling center offers distinct advantages to a community. It can offer extended counseling and psychotherapy that most pastors are not equipped for and haven't the time for. It is one place for referral. And it is an additional way to minister to those without a church home, another "half-way house" mission of service to the world.

Can the ministries of extended formal counseling and parish leadership be combined? One minister with a clinical doctorate in psychology, employed half-time as a pastor, solved that conflict-of-interest dilemma by working in a center away from her own parish. She would see parishioners without charge as many as three or four times along the patterns set up by any good pastor. She would not, however, see her own parishioners and on a free-for-service basis over an extended time. They would be referred. That arrangement seems altogether appropriate and wise. Parishioners must be seen as part of the congregation, not prospective clients for one's extra remunerative employment in pastoral counseling.

Notes

1. William Harold Tiemann, *The Right to Silence* (Richmond: John Knox Press, 1964).

2. Ibid., pp. 31-32.

3. The *Omaha World-Herald*, September 24, 1982.

4. Sissela Bok, *Lying* (New York: Random House, 1978), pp. 227-42.

5. Ibid., p. 149.

6. Ibid., p. 247.

7. Janet F. Fishburn, "Male Clergy Adultery as Vocational Confusion," *The Christian Century* 99 (September 15-22, 1982): 923.

8. "Sexual Contact by Pastors and Pastoral Counselors in Professional Relationships" (Seattle: Washington Association of Churches, 1984).

9. Bok, *Lying*, ch. 3.

6.

FINANCING MINISTRY

Every human community has an economic dimension. The church is no exception. Thus if we ask with Stanley Hauerwas "what kind of a community the church must be to rightly tell the stories of God,"[1] we will ask the question not only of our preaching and polity and pastoral care, but of money matters as well. How does the church appropriately finance its ministry?

Fortunately, money making has become less intrusive a goal for clergy than for many other professional groups. In some cases, an occupation's "code of ethics" is little more than a system of professional protectionism and mutual back-scratching for the upgrading not so much of service as of income.

Money is a means to an end. In a market economy, however, money is so pervasively used as a measure of everything from productive efficiency or libelous injury to social status or the "worth" of art that it easily becomes an end in itself. We take it too seriously.

We do this in several ways, religiously speaking. On the one hand we may tie ourselves up in knots of guilt or ethical scrupulosity: Should we be giving away more money, and should it be here or there? On the other hand, more commonplace, we may allow an obsessive desire for more money to warp our witness to the gospel. The first commentary in an ethical reflection on money ought, perhaps, to be a vernacular shrug that says "no big deal."

AMBIGUITIES

The ambiguity of a *paid* religious ministry, with its moral norms of selfless service, has escaped the caustic pen of neither prophetic nor cynical commentators. The prophets railed against the priests. Jesus accused religious leaders among his contemporaries of practicing their piety for public acclaim, and he attacked the temple money-changers. Kierkegaard, choosing lay status, asked whether true Christianity could become a reality within established Christendom, being led as it was by church officials so well supported with social status. Any dedicated seminarian suffers the ambivalence of wanting on the one hand to be a nonacquisitive servant of Word and church and of wondering, on the other, whether she or he will be able, on a typical clerical income, to make ends meet for self and family.

Our ordaining language about ministry is idealistic. The minister is "set apart"—as if from a questionable kind of wage-earning activity that ordinary men and women must pursue. And the congregation, sometimes with the financial help or prodding persuasion of its denomination, undertakes financial support for that minister as if to replace the loss of a "regular" kind of income from the normal sources of honest toil.

The ambiguity then follows. Is the salary to be seen as a payment for professional services or a gift to allow for this unique pursuit? How is the salary to be set? By considering the required graduate level of training for the profession, which is comparable to that of the lawyer? According to what the parish church can manage to raise in funds, whether minimal or lavish? According to need ("She has a well-paid husband, so she won't need much.")? According to what the market will bear? According to what will suffice to secure adequate pastoral leadership? Or that amount, perhaps, subtracting what the pastor's self-help earnings in fees and honoraria are expected to be?

The Internal Revenue Service colludes in this muddle by stipulating that upward of a third of the ordained minister's income may be considered nontaxable as a "housing allowance," as if privately selected housing were still for the convenience of, and at the requirement of, the employer as the old next-to-the-church parsonage certainly was. Ministers' pay is special. (There has even been a double deduction. Interest and real estate taxes, paid from within this nontaxable allowance, can be subtracted from Federal income tax again!)

Language that puts the clergy into a special moral category apart from financial responsibilities comparable to those of the laity is not only theologically suspect, it can be harmful practically. Pretty as the phrase may be, "setting the minister apart" for selfless service can provide a congregation the rationale for subsistence-level clergy salaries, a level that interferes with the work of ministry by all but the rare saints among us. Irrationally idealistic language also creates guilt and repressed (or open) resentment that likewise conflict with good pastoral leadership. Special clergy privileges also create lay resentments.

At root, the "set-apart" language participates in a scheme of thought that creates a double standard of morality and piety. It is as if the call and the gift of God to all Christians were something less than the call and the gift of God to a special class, the ordained. To the contrary, *all* Christians are called to deal responsibly and generously with their power to earn, with their ability to serve, and with the income from their occupational pursuits. The minister is no exception. All Christians are, or ought to be, free to negotiate a fair wage, and free to leave a job when it does not seem best as a way to invest their talent and to meet such responsibilities as marriage and child rearing.

In short, all people should be supported in any work of life that society wants done—whether street cleaner or state legislator, whether caregiver for infants or physician for heart patients. And all Christians are called to the task of learning to live free from the enslavements of acquisitiveness, overweening financial ambition, and consumerism. The efficiency-building advantages of a market system, with its considerable discrepancies of income from one sector to another, do not negate this principle. In the abstract, the moral justification for wage level differentiation is in its incentive. Different wage and salary scales operate to assure society that there will be enough physicians, truckdrivers, entrepreneurs, or ministers. The other rationales, by which one group or another claims a higher monetary "worth" than another, are deeply questionable on Christian grounds. To each person, as person, there are owed the necessities of life, a livelihood (e.g., cf. Matt. 20:1-16).

Our approach in this book is not so much reformist as consultative, but a thoughtful ethic must keep the imagination alive. There are other options for financing ministry, with a richer moral base than our own. It would be easy to suggest that biblical and theological arguments favor abandoning competitive and hierarchical bases for salary allotments altogether. Ever since its formation twenty-odd years ago, the Lutheran Church of Australia has paid all its clergy the same—rural and urban, small-church and large, assistant and senior. (Increments are given for children.) William Hulme attributes some significant findings to that remunerative system. In response to the statement, "Higher salaries would improve the lot of clergy," 77 percent of the Australian Lutheran pastors said no, compared to 46.6 percent of a similar American sample. Although they are not as well paid as Americans, fewer than a quarter of the Australians thought higher salaries were needed; 56 percent of the Americans did. What Hulme sees here is a "liberation from the financial discontent that our cultural values constantly generate."[2]

MOONLIGHTING AND TENT MAKING

The apostle Paul wrote that he had a right to food and drink, and even to be accompanied by a wife, had he been married (I Cor. 9:4-5). "Who serves as a soldier," he asked, "at his own expense?" (9:7). Paul cites the temple tradition of support for the priests and even a commandment of the Lord that is otherwise unknown to us (9:13-14). But Paul then reports to the Corinthians that he has not made use of that right! He is a part-time tentmaker. He moonlights (I Cor. 4:12, 9:15; Acts 18:3; II Thess. 3:7-8).

In many middle-class churches, professional standards and personal identity for the pastor have demanded full-time work. "The minister therefore gives himself completely to his profession. . . . To engage for a certain part of his time in other remunerative work would, he believes, break into the usefulness of his calling."[3] Lutherans require that a pastor accept employment beyond the congregation's life only with the consent of that congregation or the bishop or both, and that no fees in addition to salary be required for special pastoral services.

Some congregations and denominational pension boards have had a hard time adjusting to part-time clergy. Yet there are numerous precedents—the many New England farmers who were also pastors; great numbers of low-income Black churches whose pastors have held secular weekday jobs; the obvious cases of small parishes that offer low stipends and yet ask for fully educated ministers; and the more recent instances of theologically trained couples who choose a joint ministry and joint child rearing and home making.

For two major reasons, tent making and supplementary work loads should be undertaken only after careful moral consideration. The first is the obvious problem with the professional "contract" of availability already discussed. If one's pastor is off selling shoes or practicing law, the parishioner is hesitant to seek ministry even if told to call at any time. If the tent making is of such a sort that more time for it means more money, it creates an ever present temptation to skimp on church work for the sake of extra hours at sewing canvas.

117

The other issue for professional ethics is more profound. Certain kinds of second jobs create unwarranted conflicts of interest. Professionals, including clergy, live daily with potential conflicts of interest and they do not need more of them. The part-time minister who is also part-time home-maker or writer can usually manage pastoral responsibility with assurance, or at least without professional ethical compromise. But the one who begins to sell insurance or real estate in the community inevitably begins to view people not only as parishioners or potential parishioners, but as sales prospects also. With that influence on the relationship, pastoral care and prophetic counsel are warped. It is a shift in perspective analogous to that of the counselor who begins to date a counselee, meanwhile expecting to continue as psychotherapist for the same person.

The combination of modest salaries and personal financial ambition has enticed many young clergy into compromises of these principles, some of them sad indeed. During his first ten years of ministry, one young pastor earned a Doctorate of Ministry and moved to a much larger congregation with added responsibilities. He was pleased with his increased income, but he still felt the pinch because of added family responsibilities. He then checked the inflation index and

The shock, he wrote, led to other questions. "How big a church was I going to have to take next time? How many churches like that are there? Do I want to be professionally restricted by a larger church?" Financial ambition led to the distressing compromise shortly thereafter, as evidenced in a letter written to seminarians. "God does provide . . . . God has given me an opportunity to be making $10,000 to $15,000 . . . this year on a part-time basis. It is a business cooperative venture with other professionals helping people to help themselves . . . . I would like to telephone you and see if we could get together soon and talk about economic diversification in your future." He was involved in an exploitative pyramid franchise and sales scheme.

THE EROSION OF CLERGY PAY

There are increasing numbers of ordained ministers and priests who not only have adequate resources of their own but are willing to offer their services gratis to the congregations and the wider church. They and the "hyphenated priests" (the lawyer-priest, for example, the worker-priest, the teacher-priest) need to be aware not only of the church's appreciation for this double theological and fiduciary gift of theirs, but also of the problem they can create if they use it irresponsibly.

One man who was an heir to an industrial fortune, one of the ablest preachers in his region, served a congregation for years without pay—an ecclesiastical dollar-a-year professional. Upon his departure, that congregation struggled for several more years gathering resources for a feasible institutional life. The pastor's well-meant generosity had handicapped them. Had he invested more thought near the end of his career in that parish, channeling his giving increasingly through other agencies of the wider church and building better stewardship in the local congregation, he could have helped the congregation avoid the problem.

The problem of erosion in clergy pay rests with responsible laity fully as much as with clergy. Especially now that far more women clergy are entering the field, an exploitative salary scale, owing to the availability of more ministry candidates for less pay, is likely to evolve. Responsible church leadership, clergy and lay, will keep an eye on the larger issues. Once more, justice calls for a leadership that uses free-market negotiation as a helpful but not ultimate criterion of price and wage structure.

FEES AND HONORARIA

A related matter for ethical reflection comes with the first payment of fees and honoraria to the newly ordained. Social custom brings fees for weddings, funerals, even baptisms in some traditions, from members and nonmembers alike. To whom does the money belong? For a truly full-time parson, the money results from labor "on company time." Is it a personal gift, or payment for professional service? (It *is* taxable, if kept.) Does a fee compromise one's independence, in deciding, for example, whom to marry and whom to turn away? (Not for a good professional.)

Practice in the matter of fees is so varied that any hard and fast rules would smack of moralism. Not a few clergy, in light of their commitment to the congregation (and to deflate congregational rumors about how much the minister makes from fees?), give their fees to the church's general or benevolence budget. In parsonages of my childhood, the fees were widely given to the (male) pastor's wife! Some clergy do not accept fees. Others do, but only from nonmembers. And others see little problem at all in pocketing fees as supplementary professional support. Some even stipulate their charges, particularly to funeral directors, who then collect the fee from the bereaved. Those who accept fees are obligated to good record keeping, for tax purposes.

Even though we cannot specify a code, fees merit our ethical reflection. We must ask what our practices say to the world. We must avoid even the appearance of simony, as if the blessing of God could be bought. We must always make allowance for those who cannot pay. And we must guide the congregation, lest it set inflexibly high costs for use of the church building and staff and offend rather than serve. Such guidance requires both tact and firmness with families who are spending literally thousands of dollars on wedding festivities and yet begrudge modest payments for extra time from organists or custodians.

We need to remember that there is genuine befuddlement among many laypeople, too. "How much should we tip the minister?" asked one bride's mother of her friend on the church council. She might have been helped had the church already established broad guidelines for members and nonmembers.

One caution and one suggestion may follow from all this: If

a pastor finds himself or herself counting heavily on fees for income, there is danger ahead. The professional goal is service to the increase of faith and hope and love. Any fees and honoraria must take a very incidental place in the planning of our work according to these larger norms, if they take any place at all. As for the suggestion, let us urge congregations to think through the matter of fees and provide guidance in printed materials that are easily available.

GUIDELINES

Relatively few full-time pastors now live, as many did during the depressed time of the Mueller and Hartshorne study, below the poverty level. Nonetheless, clergy pay is low, by professional standards. Even adding the housing provided, graduating seminarians often begin full-time work at something less than that of a beginning schoolteacher or machinist, and they may be strapped as well by heavy educational loan repayments. However, to cite a different yardstick, chances are strong that the pastor's income is not below what at least a third of the parishioners themselves are trying to live on. Most readers, of course, can cite notorious exceptions.

The weight of argument, therefore, hinges on the propriety of the present pattern. Is the church's mission subverted because the clergy, especially in marginal churches, are underpaid by one measure or another? What are the right measures? (Poets and artists, certainly contributors of the human good and deserving by the standards of creativity and education, often survive on very meager income. Some lawyers start lower than clergy—some much higher—but their long-term financial prospects are decidedly better.) What responsibility has the minister to work for change in the present pattern—to join a clergy "union" for example, or to push locally at least for larger salary benefits?

Whatever the answers to such questions, the following

guidelines seem appropriate. (1) The minister and ministerial couple should enter ministry for its intrinsic worth as a calling, hoping to receive an "institutional call" in the form of an assignment in ministry, with income enough to be free for that ministry. They should not elect ministry anticipating that this occupational pursuit will set them financially above that of most other breadwinners, or because of its inherent prestige. (Empirically speaking, the ordained ministry is an avenue of upward mobility for a very sizable percentage of clergy candidates.)

(2) The minister should cultivate the graces that enable a person to live simply, without undue jealousy of those who are better off—obviously far easier said than done. This is simply a virtue that ought to be part of any Christian life-style. (There is further comment around this theme in the final section of this chapter.)

(3) The minister should at the same time support a strong salary base for clergy. This is a matter of justice and effectiveness and self-respect rather than self-aggrandizement. The Christian does defend family and neighbor, while playing down assertions of personal right.

This set of guidelines arises from prudential considerations if nothing else. The seminarian entering ministry with neither savings, independent income, nor strong family financial backing is well advised to cultivate the arts and economies of frugal living. There is a broader consideration as well. In a throw-away consumer society, we hear a moral call to the simple life, as well as to the devout and holy one. Congruence between our teaching of good personal stewardship and public concern for both the present environment and the planet's future resources is incumbent on us just as professional congruence mandates that physicians and nurses not smoke once they begin teaching patients that smoking counteracts good health.

Yet another salient argument pertains to personal finance. The minister needs freedom to demit the ministry. The ability to survive on a low income enhances this freedom, as does a second occupational competence. The freedom is important lest one sell one's soul simply to stay on the job and take the salary when principle dictates otherwise, or pretend a faith after a genuine conversion to agnosticism.

FUND RAISING

How shall the church raise its money? In a valuable essay on applied ethical theory, "Stewardship as Promotion," James Gustafson reports on a manipulative church fund-raiser whose principle "was to find and use symbols, words, and deeds that most persuasively unleash the need to give, regardless of any ethical or theological convictions that might bring these procedures under judgment. If status-competition is what it takes, use it; if Bible quoting is what it takes, use it."[4] More damning yet, says Gustafson, "Churches raised no serious questions about this prostitution."

What kind of an institution must the church be if it is rightly to tell the stories of God? On the subject of finances, certainly, one that conducts its institutional business with integrity.

Integrity, therefore, must be our byword; congruence of ends and means. Fund raising should be straightforward and not devious, open rather than secretive. Religious efforts are given a bad name in our culture more often not by the scandal of the cross but by three things: sexual misdeeds on the part of clergy, religious insipidity, and financial fraudulence or mismanagement.

Integrity means there must be an ethics to our promotion. Legally, of course, funds must be spent on the purpose for which they are raised. Likewise, morally. Politicians are indicted when they appropriate for personal use funds that were raised for campaigning. The church or charitable foundation that advertises with pictures of starving Ethiopian babies and then uses 65 percent of the resultant income on promotion or in-house staff salaries violates that kind of norm.

Integrity avoids exploiting vulnerable people. The media

evangelists are most tempted. They do not know their donors personally. One highly problematic case was cited in chapter 1. To a widow who had been sending in sizable sums, one TV evangelist wrote: "I am your pastor. Put your trust in me." He proceeded, each time he wrote, with a new appeal for funds, and within a few years the frail and formerly well-off woman was writing to her sons, "I am out of money." She had given a half-million dollars to a TV personality.

Integrity in the interpretive materials of promotion is no small order in a society so smothered in promotional hype. Whether it is true or not, we compete for dollars, it seems, with hard-sell direct-mail appeals, and with TV's religious stars, and we are tempted to shift our style in their direction.

Integrity also means avoiding "undue influence," to use a legal term, when we are pastorally close to aging people who may be writing or rewriting their wills. As both professionals and friends of such people, we may find them seeking our counsel.

Integrity means disclosure. Beyond holding confidential the amounts given by individual donors, religious organizations have little business keeping closed books. Secrecy is too harmful to the reputation of the church even among its own members, let alone in the society at large. TV evangelists have been among the most culpable, and the founding of the Evangelical Council for Financial Accountability in 1979 was a welcome event. Each of the 207-member organizations is pledged to send an audited financial statement to anyone asking for it, whether donor or newspaper reporter. Would that all denominational offices, Catholic and Protestant, were as open. Without disclosure public trust cannot grow. Billy Graham and his staff are on salary and Graham himself reports that he has "not accepted a gift, honorarium or personal offering in at least thirty years."[5]

Fund raising with integrity means right method. The tax-exempt status of religious organizations leaves tempting loopholes for the unscrupulous. Leadership personnel in Synanon, the Church of Scientology, and the Unification

Church have all faced indictments for what the law has considered a misuse of these privileges. Generating funds from business income, *if* that business enterprise exploits exemptions given to religious organizations for religious purposes, creates a scandal. Not only is it unfair to secular competitors; it distorts the work of the church.

One group of priests supported itself through a huge mail-order business selling everything from bath oil to books on how to avoid paying taxes. They requested tax exemption on their opulent headquarters building and nonprofit mailing privileges, since they claimed religious purpose. After all, they were priests. The line between the harmless small-scale bake sale or car wash and these deceptive business projects needs to be conscientiously drawn.

Gambling is yet another moral issue in fund raising. That some states have now taken up the lottery as a means for raising revenue does not justify a similar erosion of principle in the church. We are not to play on people's weaknesses. Again, the small-scale down-home bingo game with modest prizes, attended as much for fellowship as for winnings, is to be distinguished from the highly advertised, high-stakes game that plays to the sickness of gambling addiction.

One caveat for the sake of ecumenism is in order. Well-supported congregations that inherit a tradition of proportional giving need to be slow in judging the fund-raising traditions of low-income parishes, such as bingo games and raffles. Financing does not come so easily for the latter group. Middle-class bazaars and church fairs have much the same flavor. One pastor scrupulously cancelled an annual bazaar. (He favored direct stewardship only.) He thereby killed a major source of community goodwill in his neighborhood. In spite of its touted importance, the fund-raising aspect of the fair was quite secondary.

Ministry with integrity means service without false deference to wealth. The ordained minister offers pastoral care within the congregation in response to need. This means a serious attempt to treat all persons equally, without regard to social status and financial contribution. Never wholly successful, of course, the pastor resists the demonic status-ranking system that permeates social life. Those clergy who avoid knowledge of what individual members contribute to the budget find the practice helpful in striving for such equity in pastoral care. An even larger benefit may be the freedom from money consciousness in prophetic teaching and moral counsel. It is a practice to be commended, in spite of legitimate counterarguments that knowledge of people's giving offers the pastor insight into their spiritual maturity.

CLERGY UNIONS

Over time, unionism has contributed significantly to the recognition of blue-collar labor's inherent dignity and its rights in sharing the profits of an advancing industrial economy. Nonetheless, unionism has now fallen on hard times indeed.

Unionism catches on more slowly in the white-collar and professional ranks that now constitute the major sectors of the work force. However, these workers, too, now serve employing firms more often than not. They are little more likely than miners and assembly-line workers to be found in small family enterprises or among the self-employed. Were it not for attitudes born of social class and perceived possibilities for upward mobility, they would seem to be ripe for organization.

In potential for trade association organizing, far down the line in this white-collar and professional roster—well after schoolteachers, clerk-typists, bookkeepers, flight controllers, and physicians—are the clergy. They are least likely to be organized into unions, though, it might be argued, hardly the least in need. The major reason for this, of course, is the isolation of pastors in their typical pattern of deployment. They do not work in sizable numbers for single employers. Another reason, however, is ideological. Clergy may think themselves to be above organizing. And organizing may seem unethical.

There is little reason in such a position. It is virtually an axiom in our theological understanding of sin and human society that corporate, collective groups in a society need to be represented in decisions that affect their lives. Negotiating through collective bargaining is the better route toward some semblance of justice, far better than one-way, top-down decision making. Unrepresented groups fall behind; they are made victims, even in well-meaning paternalistic structures.

Unions, of course, do not always exist by that name. Different patterns of work and support breed different types of organizations. Various guilds, like the American Medical Association or the National Education Association, serve as unions for their respective constituencies. In the more centralized denominations, despite the absence of traditional patterns of collective bargaining, the "negotiation" for minimal salaries and pension support may be a participatory process, *de facto*. Clergy unions have arisen more often in such public, nondenominational sectors as state-employed chaplaincies, paralleling nurses' or the prison guards' organizations, for example, or in hierarchical systems like the Catholic Church, when local priests feel the need of representation over and against the higher diocesan authorities.

The point in this brief discussion is simply this: The invitation to join a union or association of clergy presents less of a dilemma in professional ethics than most clergy will think. "Self-seeking" is not the goal of organization so much as participating in decisions for the sake of the long-term strength of the church's leadership and mission. Anger may be a legitimate part of the motive. Greed or exploitation of others, or of institutional vulnerabilities, is not.

Clergy unions, where they exist, can also serve as exemplars for society in a culture that has a relatively poor understanding of the participatory and collective bargaining routes to economic decision making. Call it economic democracy, analogous to political democracy. This exemplary responsibility of the church through its own organizational life-style has already been discussed in chapter 2.

127

Another dimension to the modeling role, beyond the quest for justice, has to do with enhancing professional competence. Far too many white-collar and professional trade associations fail to see one of their major responsibilities in this realm. Teachers' associations bargain for pay scale, and they manage grievance procedures, but in only very limited ways do they use their considerable power for upgrading teaching competence. Accountants, bankers, and insurance underwriters do better. A good clergy union or association will emphasize continuing education more than it does salaries and benefits.

EVALUATION AND INCREMENTS

One further aspect of the financial structure of the pastor's relationship to a congregation merits comment. Consistent with the approach in chapter 2, the minister or priest establishes an open give-and-take with parishioners about his or her own work as leader. That work is not above constructive criticism. The work of ordained ministry is but one part of the body's entire and corporate witness. Therefore interaction, "feedback" from the congregation, is theologically imperative. In secular language, this means regularly evaluating our work, performance reviews. One occasion that can prompt such consultation comes annually when one board or another considers cost-of-living and merit increments in the pastor's salary.

Most of us need explicit organizational tools for expediting this process. Most polities could profit from copying the United Methodist *Discipline*'s requirement of a Pastor-Parish Relations Committee. A denominationally provided worksheet may even be helpful to such a lay group, lest generalities and vapid compliments be the main content of an annual review session. Just which kinds of sermons are helpful? What visitation is important to laypeople, and what can be left in abeyance if time runs out? How well is the educational and missional work progressing, given the current investment of professional energies in those areas?

Another important topic in such consultation can be the pastor's own "outside" involvements, a useful catalyst for discussing the church's missional purposes. Most clergy devote a part of their energies to denominational committee work or outreach, and some part of it as well to the local community. If these commitments subtract considerable time from intraparish service, the congregation ought also to be party to the decisions.

THE SIMPLE LIFE

Modestly paid as most clergy are, it is true they need an extra measure of skill in and commitment to plain living, but on the subject of personal finances there is no essential difference in our calling from that of other Christians. Some persons in society of course are more directly involved in gathering investment capital or creating wealth through economic enterprise than others, but a simple call toward the "devout and holy life" comes to all. This aspect of our common vocation merits special emphasis in a day when so many distracting wants are created through advertising and the media, when the earth's resources for future generations are in jeopardy, and when the extent of poverty in the Third World is so great. All three of Jesus' temptations had to do with satisfying personal ambition at the expense of fidelity to God's way.

Some older assumptions about the minister's life are changing. Leiffer asked more than three thousand ministers in various samples how much they agreed with this statement: "The minister and his family should live simply and unostentatiously, regardless of the standard of living of his church members."[6] Of clergy under thirty years of age, the percentage of those agreeing or "tending to agree" with the statement was in most categories at least 25 percentage points lower than for those more than fifty-five years of age. (He assumes that the attitudes will not change markedly as this younger group ages.) In some denominations, the difference was fifty points.

We no longer live with that imminent eschatological vision of the primitive church, with its received injunctions that missioners take nothing for the journey, neither staff nor bag (Luke 9:3 and parallels), and the practice in Jerusalem that prompted converts to sell all they had as they joined the community. Most of us are not celibate, most of us do not take vows of poverty, nor are we members of a religious order that takes care of its elderly. In short, we have moral responsibilities to others and to our own future maintenance lest we become an undue burden in our later years.

We are caught up in the secular order, and we are sustained by it. We do not seek out a sectarian place called purity; it does not exist. The coin with Caesar's head is in every pocket (Luke 20:24).

Nonetheless, pastoral ethics would argue for a relatively simple life. Most clergy, of course, accept that perforce, but an intentional esteeming of it is more than rationalizing. Consumerism is a social sickness. The needs of the poor and of cultural enterprises not funded by the public sector are all reasons for generous stewardship of wealth. The Christian bias toward simplicity has a long and authoritative history. Christian trust helps free us from the compulsions that make some tight-fisted people "insurance poor" through accumulating wealth against unreasonably threatening and fantastically numerous rainy days.

There are church folk of course, both rich and poor, who want their clergy to be not only well provided for but lavishly equipped. Some parishioners want to protest their own poverty through a vicarious display of wealth by their pastors, thus raising moral dilemmas for those leaders. Turning aside gifts is often poor pastoral response, but in this instance, teaching a better stewardship would seem morally required. Those clergy who see the church more as an arena of self-employment and self-aggrandizement than a body whose witness can be strengthened through economic humility have missed part of the marrow of good pastoral ethics.

Again, however, recall this chapter's vernacular opening: "no big deal." Integrity in fund raising and solid, humble stewardship of means is all that professional ministry ethics can legislate. Urging the admirable and more stringent witness of the pastor who takes no fees, who turns over all income beyond subsistence, or who chooses on principle to work only among the rural or urban poor is beyond the scope of our present project.

Many pastors are paid adequately, and many are not. On behalf of the latter, we all have a duty of firm advocacy when it comes to discussing professional pay scales. In most American parishes, if the pastor is willing to live among the people more or less at their economic level, decent support for competent ministry is going to be available.

One of the biblical injunctions written with church leadership in mind is worth quoting at length:

> We brought nothing into the world, and we cannot take anything out of the world; but if we have food and clothing, with these we shall be content. But those who desire to be rich fall into temptation, into a snare, into many senseless and hurtful desires that plunge [us] into ruin and destruction. For the love of money is the root of all evils; it is through this craving that some have wandered away from the faith and pierced their hearts with many pangs. (I Tim. 6:7-10)

Notes

1. Stanley Hauerwas, *A Community of Character* (Notre Dame, Ind.: University of Notre Dame Press, 1981), p. 4.

2. William E. Hulme, "Pastors' Salaries," *The Christian Ministry* 16 (November 1985): 4.

3. Nolan B. Harmon, Jr., *Ministerial Ethics and Etiquette* (Nashville: Cokesbury Press, 1928), p. 25.

4. James Gustafson, "The Ethics of Promotion: Stewardship as Promotion," in *Stewardship in Contemporary Life*, ed. T. K. Thompson (New York: Association Press, 1965), pp. 154-55.

5. "Sex and Money," *The Christian Century* 100 (August 17-24, 1983): 738.

6. Murray H. Leiffer, *Changing Expectations and Ethics in the Professional Ministry* (Evanston: Garrett Theological Seminary, 1969), p. 33.

7.

RELATIONSHIPS WITH OTHER CLERGY

Karen Duval has recently left her first five-year assignment in parish ministry. She has taken a position with larger responsibilities in an urban congregation sixty-five miles away. Karen did an outstanding job at St. Andrews, helping it to grow in both spirit and membership. Eighty-five new members were added to the rolls; many of them were young couples who said they had always wanted a church like St. Andrews and a minister like Karen Duval. One such couple, Sue and Robert Koenig, were among Karen's closest friends.

Now a call has come from Robert. Robert's father, a marginal member of St. Andrews, a man who only rarely attended church, has been killed in an automobile accident. The Koenigs were a close clan, and Robert is devastated. He needs pastoral support. Karen knows not only that Michael Johnson, her successor at St. Andrews, is new on the job, but also that he will be a hard person for Sue and Robert to come to know and trust. He is reserved and slow in reaching out, a trifle dour. Sue and Robert still think of Karen as their pastor and confidante. In fact, they have visited Karen's new congregation for worship three times in as many months.

Karen wants to be of help to these close friends and former parishioners in their grief, yet she doesn't feel just right about going back to call on them. Important as her caring is, acting on it seems to violate an assumed obligation to Michael Johnson.

Professional life requires ethical concern for relationships with one's peers. Many codes of ethics make this matter their primary concern. Some students of the professions—Durkheim, Tawney, and Parsons for example—see this as a useful and altruistic effort. The professional guild stands over against the extreme individualism of *laissez-faire*. It also represents an independent source of influence and power over against the authoritarianism of a collectivist society with its concentration of control in the hands of the state or an economic oligarchy.

Others, like C. Wright Mills, would point rather to the monopolistic and technocratic tendency in the professional associations themselves. These writers offer a far less optimistic understanding of this careful deference to one another within the colleague group. Of late, our courts of law have taken the less sanguine view in at least one respect. Seeing the practice as a restraint of trade, they have ruled that bar and medical associations must stop prohibiting advertising by their members.

Highly professional groups also exercise control over the educational and licensing gateways into their respective fields. They rationalize as altruistic this regulating of the gateway, just as they do the other parts of their codes. One writer sums up the issue well by stating his ambivalence about the role of the professional groups: "Janus-headed, they promise both a structural basis for a free and independent citizenry in a world threatened by bureaucratic tyranny and at the same time themselves harbour a threat to freedom."[1]

Sociological and theological skepticism about professional virtue should provoke in us enough self-awareness that we keep alert to ways that our codes create a subtle collusion against outsiders for reasons of mere self-interest. Through our pastoral "ethics" we may be holding back emerging lay leadership, for example, or we may be resisting relatively new groups like women, who want to enter ordained ministry. Peer loyalties in our professional codes must usually be affirmed, but with a salty bit of moral suspicion all the while.

RELATIONS TO SUCCESSORS

When asked what problems pastoral ethics should address, judicatory people and pastors alike name "meddling" as the most troublesome of all. They speak of continued involvement by a minister or priest in the affairs of a congregation after he or she has left. This is probably the issue most in need of commonly enforced rules in ministry ethics. Karen Duval is right in sensing an obligation to Michael Johnson.

The ministry codes are explicit. Says one, "I will refrain from speaking disparagingly about the work of either my predecessor or my successor. . . . I will never embarrass my successor by meddling in the affairs of the church I formerly served."[2]

Pressures to contravene this policy are quite understandable. Pastoral relationships are deeply personal, as Karen Duval knows, and invitations or requests addressed to former pastors seem altogether natural to a church member. The person may intend no slight whatever to an incumbent in the local pastorate. Unfortunately, the former pastor may not appreciate the magnitude of the intrusion that accepting such an invitation presents.

A commonplace and especially difficult case relates to the retiring minister. One can think of pitiful situations in which the retiring minister's own sense of human worth and identity hinges heavily on the pastoral status. If that minister stays on in a neighborhood near enough to be accessible to or active in the last congregation, the pressures flood in, coming both from parishioners and the retired pastor alike. It is at this point that I have found the most anger from clergy I have interviewed. Little wonder that the issue is often virtually a centerpiece of clergy ethics essays. Ministers speak of their work being made more difficult by the "interference" and "meddling" and even "plotting" of former pastors. The Presbyterian *Book of Order* is explicit therefore: "Former pastors of a congregation may officiate at services for members thereof, or at services within its properties, only upon invitation from the moderator thereof."[3]

What is at issue here? If Karen Duval is a caring and humane pastor, committed to serving the deepest spiritual needs of people who come to her, how can she turn away a request for meaningful service? The reasons rest with our definition of "client" for the ordained minister. The minister is not simply a private chaplain to individuals. Before that, and taking priority, we are bonded to and seek the welfare of the church. It is the church that ordains us, not a collection of individuals who ascribe ministry office to us and ask us for our help.

Pastor and congregation are knit together in a set of subtle interpersonal relationships, among them the relations of clergy authority, religious teaching, pastoral care, and priestly office. Attention to these relationships is a particularly high priority during the early months of a new pastorate. Any predecessor's interference with them, even for the sake of personal friendships and apparently overwhelming pastoral responsibility, must be seen as a breach of good professional ethics and a violation of our best insights into this "client" relationship. Karen Duval's inclination, let us hope, lies where her duty does, to help her successor in building his new pastoral relationships. She will have to explain this to Robert and Sue, and it cannot be easy.

These arguments should not be taken in support of an often heard assertion that a minister or priest cannot have close friends within a congregation. We do not neatly define pastoral relationships by mechanical systems of role and function. The ministry covenant is more wholesome, more organic, more fluid. This rule of nonmeddling is not a mere legalism; it stems from the overriding concern for the church.

As an institution the church on occasion will yield its formal interests to overriding personal needs. So the rule will have its exceptions. The professional needs wisdom in weighing the demands on one side and the other. Karen Duval has the right instinct in her puzzlement. She may, of course, participate in a service, if asked by the new minister at St. Andrews. Let us hope she will. She may certainly visit the Koenigs as their friend.

An Alban Institute newsletter emphasizes the arguments around this issue by listing a full ten ways that continuing contacts by former clergy influence a congregation negatively. Written by Joan Mabon, these comments are worth quoting in full, and I list them here with the Institute's permission:[4]

1. Contacts continue to resurface for members whatever negative emotions were present at the pastor's departure. *Regret:* "It's not like it used to be." *Inadequacy:* "He left us for a better church." *Guilt:* "Why didn't I do enough to make him stay?" *Anger:* "Why did he leave us flat?" *Loneliness:* "I miss her." *Frustration:* "If he were here, I could cope." *Relief:* "I'm glad he's gone and we don't have to do *that* anymore!"

2. Contacts deny members the opportunity to work through those emotions of grief directly and constructively and encourage their futile grappling with ghosts.

3. Contacts discourage members' working through their feelings within the community ("I'd better not tell my deacon that I called the old pastor.") and encourage a rivalry among members ("The pastor called *me!*").

4. Private contacts with individuals deprive the community of the opportunity to share grief and loneliness, to build the strength that comes from shared suffering, to discover resurrection hope that emerges from shared struggles.

5. Contacts focus member energy outside the congregation at a time when that energy may be needed most within the community.

6. Private communications encourage "holding on" to the past and fighting former battles—but this time with the invisible contenders; they decrease a person's ability to struggle with present realities and diminish hope for the future.

7. Contacts confuse persons as to where and how to direct their commitment to new leadership; they make that difficult task even more difficult for members.

8. Each contact places the resident pastor in the awkward position of interloper. Interim specialists are trained to deal with the negativism so that the installed pastor can begin positive building at the earliest opportunity.

9. By surfacing implicit comparisons between new and old, contacts undermine the choice of a new pastor and inhibit a wholehearted commitment to the new relationship.

10. Contacts keep the new pastor on the defensive and subvert that pastor's morale and effectiveness. The new pastor can never successfully compete with the old pastor's enshrined "ghost" as long as that ghost is actively present.

COMPETITION

One code begins its section called, "My Relationship to Other Ministers" with this succinct statement: "I will refuse to enter into unfair competition with other ministers in order to secure a pulpit or place of honor." It closes the same section by stating, "I will consider all ministers my co-laborers in the work of Christ and even though I may differ from them I shall respect their Christian earnestness and sincerity."[5]

Inevitably, clergy do compete in many subtle ways on behalf of a congregation and for personal satisfaction and advancement. Part of the dynamic in the American religious scene arises from this competition. The same dynamism, however, can also hinder the mission of the church and become a scandal that mocks the unity we have in Christ. Thus, there are persuasive theological reasons for these elements in the codes; they do more than undergird a you-scratch-my-back-I'll-scratch-yours collusion.

Foremost among these reasons is the ecumenical imperative. Believing that we are all one in Christ, there being neither male nor female, slave nor free, Presbyterian nor Methodist, we do strive for less animosity within the

Christian family. As pastors, we are engaged in the common effort, alongside other clergy, to advance the cause of Christ. We do not steal sheep from one another. We are called on to encourage and affirm, not denigrate, the work of other pastors.

As a case in point, a nearby pastor takes a public stance on abortion—or prayer in the schools, or nuclear weapons, or a local labor dispute—with which I disagree. My temptation is to call that pastor incompetent or ill-informed, biased, or misguided. My obligation, however, is to assume that the stance is a sincere attempt at ministry and witness, and to provide within the diverse Christian family my own theological testimony for an opposing position.

In another case, I call upon a new family in a community. My temptation is to "sell" my own church as a fit place for that family to find a church home, and to play down the gifts of other congregations, yet I resist the sales-pitch image. It seems to boast and to divide the Body of Christ.

My obligation as I call on newcomers is to welcome them into the community in the name of Christ, to inform them about the community's religious life, and to offer help for working into that life as meaningfully as possible. We are not to demean the gospel and the church by hawking our wares like competitive salespeople after their private commissions. Least of all should we belittle other congregations and their clergy. At this point, even if for different reasons, our charge is like such other canons as that of the engineers, whose code includes provisions like these: "[It is professionally unethical] to attempt to injure falsely or maliciously, directly or indirectly, the professional reputation, prospects, or business of another engineer . . . to advertise in self-laudatory language, or in any other manner derogatory to the dignity of the profession."

Some pastors, concerned for denominational loyalty, also recommend careful referrals by tradition. If as a Methodist, I encounter a new Lutheran family in town, I call the nearest Lutheran pastor with that information. Presbyterians, they say, "belong" to the Presbyterian pastor of their new community, Baptists to the Baptist. That position has some virtue. Certainly, denominational options in the new community are a part of the information I share in my welcome to the new family. However, one of the great realities of the ecumenical movement, hierarchical resistance notwithstanding, is the regular traffic of laypeople from one

ECUMENICAL ETHICS

We are speaking, then, of "ecumenical ethics." When people from one congregation visit another, for example, it is unethical aggressively to woo them away from a congregation in which there are no clear reasons for their inactivity or alienation. A healthy movement to appropriate congregations is to be expected in a society as open as ours, but "sheep stealing" has long been despised, and for good reason.

One church member, uncomfortable with the inclusive language being introduced into his own congregation's pattern of worship, spent several weeks in the prayer meetings of an Assembly of God nearby, and absented himself from his own church. When he came back to regular participation in his home church, he told someone a story of ecumenical ethics, from an unanticipated source. "That Assemblies pastor and I got together for prayer one time, and he said to me that night: 'Hank, go back to your church! God wants you there. He has work for you to do! Go back. And study your Bible. Study, study, study.' And that's what I've tried to do."

At the time a person wants to move from one congregation to another of a different tradition, notification through a request for a letter of transfer from the new congregation is in order, even if the change is from Catholic to Protestant. Clearly, the response will not always be as routine as it is from sister churches within the same denomination. It may not materialize in some instances, but the gesture of ecumenical spirit is worth the effort. If such a request is

140

received, the gracious pastor will accommodate it without rancor, quite possibly after seeing the person making the transfer and wishing him or her well.

Membership is far from the most important issue in ecumenical ethics. Consider, for example, the so-called Lima Document from the Faith and Order Commission of the World Council of Churches. It had the concurrence of several Roman Catholic theologians who participated in the drafting. *Baptism, Eucharist, and Ministry*, as it is called, has implications for interdenominational relationships that can be interpreted in professional terms. About baptism, for example, the document states: "Baptism is an unrepeatable act. Any practice which might be interpreted as 're-baptism' must be avoided."[6] "Re-baptism" would denigrate a partner-servant and partner-church in the gospel.

Ordination is at present an issue more complex. "Resumption of ordained ministry requires the assent of the Church, but no reordination."[7] This text assumes resuming ministry within the same denomination. It carries implications, however, for receiving an ordained minister from another tradition. We shall be taking a giant ecumenical step forward when most denominations recognize clergy ordained before rather than ordaining them again. (This is the practice among a number of Protestant communions already.) They will simply receive such clergy who are changing traditions, asking now an affirmation of a new loyalty to denominational authority and polity, but avoiding implications of "new and improved" as would a TV advertisement. "Re-ordination" has been done too frequently in these denominational changes. Deliberate efforts are needed, says the Lima Document, toward the mutual recognition of ministries. Indeed they are.

Were church language and church teaching thoroughly "low" in their treatment of ordination, if ordination were simply like being inducted into political office among the whole *laos* and nothing more, repeated ordination would be legitimate. However, the ruling theological consensus makes of the ordained clergy a different "order" of ministry and

141

therefore ecumenism is forwarded by fully accepting the status from another denomination.

THE ASSISTANT, THE ASSOCIATE, AND THE INTERIM

Ask judiciary officials about professional ethics and you are likely to hear another concern almost as regularly as the "meddling" one described earlier. It is the misdeeds, as they see it, of assistant, associate, or interim pastors who misread affection and esteem as proof of a call to become senior pastors in the churches they are serving. Affection and esteem should not be so read.

With interims, the Presbyterian *Book of Order* hedges but remains useful: "[The ministry committee of Presbytery] shall counsel with the proposed interim pastor and the session in order to make clear the expectation that this relationship should not normally lead toward a call to the pastorate of that congregation."[8] A document from one Episcopal diocese is hard and fast: "[An agreement with an interim should cover] the understanding that the interim pastor is not and will under no circumstances be a candidate for the position."[*]

One may ask, does such policy not exclude the Spirit from the lively chemistry of a leader and congregation as they work together? Long experience leads to the rules, experience that has seen too many churches divided because of a short-cut in normal process.

Selection. Begin with the short-cut problem. Choosing a pastor should be the result of a careful and deliberate search by a committee that fully represents a congregation, or by the alternative processes in more hierarchical denominations. Selecting interim ministers and assistants, and even associate pastors, is usually much simpler, and the candidate *can* therefore be much less of an ideal match than otherwise.

Division. More importantly, the assistant or interim, even though not having been thought of as a pastoral candidate by

142

many in the church, becomes a cherished pastor to some. If candidacy is not clearly out of the question, these people quite naturally begin to urge this pastor on the whole church. If they are rebuffed, they are at very least disgruntled, and they may become a strong and disaffected group. If they win out, other parties in the church may square off on the opposite side of the issue. They did not find the interim so lovable, or they have definite reservations. They may not have been represented in the original selection process.

Ambition. The candidate himself or herself sees things going smoothly; people are supportive; the community feeling is fine. Why not stay put and move up? Again, if the expectations are not clear, even when the candidate is far from being the best match the church could make through the regular appointive or search process, the candidate's natural ambition makes for self-deception. The church comes to be "courted" by that interim or associate in a way that short-circuits the regular process.

What should be done in the exceptional cases, when the Spirit does seem to dictate a placement, when there is a congregation unanimous in wanting to make this candidate the pastor? In the case of the interim, one good procedure, valuable because it honors the important concerns detailed above, is for the interim to resign. Then the congregation can spend some time with another interim, complete the deliberate search, and call the interim back, if that is its wish, and if the interim is still available. The distancing should have been helpful to both parties.

When a senior minister leaves, in the vast majority of cases it is proper for the associate or assistant to begin planning a move. In some polities, however, the position of the *associate* is carefully defined; that person has a covenant with the church and can remain on in the same role without needing to move.

COLLEAGUESHIP

There are positive resources in professional colleagueship that should now be stressed. By formal definition, the professional links his or her life with colleagues by being part of a group that monitors professional practice. The professional cannot be a loner who devises a private style of practice, indifferent to colleagues like a stereotypical idiosyncratic, avant-garde expressionist painter. We affirm individual creativity, of course; ego-centered disdain for the gifts and cares of colleagues—both ordained and lay—we do not. Christians, so aware of the community in Christ, can dismiss colleagueship least of all.

Theologian Gordon Kaufman stresses the communal nature of human life when he writes about the culture shock of a Mennonite who becomes an urban professional. Such a person leaves behind a compact rural religious community that has been close to the Bible. The inherited Mennonite ethics, which prescribed the cultural patterns back home, are an inadequate resource, says Kaufman, for confronting the decisions a lawyer, social worker, or business executive must now make. Kaufman argues that the answer is not to throw out the Bible and the whole communal Mennonite tradition, often as that happens. The Mennonite can still hold on to three things: a conviction that human life is primarily communitarian; that communal life can and should be built, even in the city, difficult as that is; and that this urban life, too, is "under God."[9]

For the modern professional, the Bible offers no prepackaged answers to scores of problems that must be faced in work life. We need a "community of discernment" to help with that. There is a long Christian tradition for such community colleagueship. It is usually in community that religious resources and the Bible come alive. Christians have traditionally said that the Spirit creates community, and that the Spirit through community interprets the Word to us. The present-day "base communities" of Latin America are a striking case in point.

The Christian professional needs a community of colleagues for a conscientious praxis in light of new occasions and new duties. Today's moral dilemmas cannot be dealt with by dint of proof texts from the Bible or by a closed religious tradition from a former cultural setting. The beauty of professional life is that such a colleagueship is both the expected norm and usually something relatively easy to establish.

The colleagueship of the ordained ministry needs to take form not only on the formal scale, such as in denominational standards for its clergy. It needs to happen at the local level as well. As he comes to St. Andrews where Karen Duval used to serve, Michael Johnson should very early find other clergy knocking on his door with collegial words of welcome. Lacking that, he should himself reach out to others.

Michael should be able to give several reasons for building a ministerium or clergy study group. *Discernment* is one. Breadth of judgment and continual reflection are expected norms for the professional. Shared wisdom helps each of us toward that end, and we owe help in turn to our colleagues. Across the country, hundreds of lectionary study groups, prayer cells, and issues-oriented discussion circles leaven the ministry in ways most of us barely guess. Clergy support groups are particularly important for women, who hold a minority status now.

Resisting burnout is a second professional imperative that begs for colleagueship. Close-knit support groups whose members can relax and trust one another can help.

Unemployment and retirement are times when colleagues can also offer one another extra support. Thinking of clergy retirement, Roy Oswald, of the Alban Institute staff, once likened clergy retirement to accounts of voodoo death, incidents in which a tribal member is punished for breaking a taboo. When the witch doctor points a magic bone at the offender, so strong are the psychic expectations that the one who is "boned" writhes in agony, crawls off to an out-of-the-way place and, shortly, dies. Oswald argued that loneliness for the newly retired could injure both morale and physical health. Retirees can easily be "boned." As professionals, we owe colleagueship to our seniors in the calling.

Imaginative, caring congregations will find various ways to honor retired clergy in their midst. The methods cannot be put in a code. Imaginative, sensitive pastors may for example invite retired clergy to lead chapel communions, to visit the sick, or to occasionally preach.

Mentoring and teaching younger colleagues has also been part of professional standards from the time of Hippocrates. Conscientious supervision of field education students, interns, and summer seminarians is the fortunate responsibility of not a few pastors, especially those located near theological schools.

Once novices pass out of student status, surveillance of younger associates demands extra tact. Whether administratively on the same staff or in some other parish, the less experienced person is now to be respected as a colleague, even while being coached. The rich relations of mentoring can create special distress when, at least for males, there comes the time that the younger person throws off the idealized elder and rebels, "becoming one's own man."[10] The mentor's resentment or possessiveness at such a season, natural as it may be, is too shallow a response, lacking insight.

Ecumenism is yet another reason for building clergy colleague networks. Interdenominational clergy groups provide small expressions of Christian unity. They offer special gifts for professional development and competence as well. The worth of what we learn from one another across the different strains of Christian tradition warrants considerable effort at building colleague groups.

Standard-setting. The joint efforts that enhance mutual trust and affection are also resources for establishing helpful professional standards. Sixty-three clergy in one California community—Catholic, Protestant, Orthodox, and Jewish—set minimal requirements for premarital counseling: a four-month waiting period for marriage, two premarital counseling sessions, and instruction also from a mature lay couple.

REFERENCES

Jeremy Brinton was on the pastoral search committee. He was intent on checking out references by telephone. He knew that most written references lack candor about negative traits in candidates.

Brinton spent virtually an entire day tracking down and interviewing five persons concerning a prospective assistant minister, Clayton Poyner. Three of the references were ordained persons themselves. There were no negative comments forthcoming in the whole day of consultation. Clayton was hired.

Within a year it became clear that Clayton was a young man who did not pay his bills, had trouble keeping appointments, and was inept in some broader areas of ministry as well. He was not an adequate role model for younger people. His wife was subject to chronic depression and was suicidal—a very heavy drain on Poyner's own work and on the church's caring energies.

Jeremy concluded that Clayton Poyner was inappropriate for the ministry, at least *this* ministry. He was by this time so frustrated that he invested more time calling back the very references he had spoken to a year earlier. He was both angry and inquisitive. Had they known about Clayton's problems? The gist of the reaction from four of the five was simply this: "Yes, but we didn't want to hurt his future."

In our references and recommendations pertaining to personnel placement, we need to reflect a loyalty to the larger good of an institution as well as a sensitive concern for individuals. Jeremy Brinton's parish church was significantly set back in its service and witness. Clayton's extra months of employment (he was terminated after one year) did not help him solve his problems. Indeed, those problems were made worse by an additional employment failure. He should have moved to a different line of work earlier. His colleagues or his denominational system should have offered counseling and vocational coaching. Candid openness on the part of his references might have helped. Brinton's anger interfered with what his own committee might have done in support for Clayton's vocational and personal problems. The obligations of colleagueship among the clergy were misunderstood by the referees.

An analogous problem, probably more common, arises in the case of alcoholism. Candor is among the moral obligations of "tough love" that we owe our colleagues. We are to maintain honest relationships, not false ones. The earlier we can help the genuine alcoholic admit the problem and seek the right kind of help, the better.

A related problem, of course, is the matter of resources to help the emotionally troubled pastor. Deployment officers like judicatory executives ought to understand the nature of confidential counseling help for clergy, but they often do not. Repeatedly we hear of such administrators asking denominationally provided counselors for professional evaluations of the clergy they counsel. Those counselors cannot provide that assessment, of course, without a breach in the very relationship that has been designed for the healing and growth of the ministers in question.

Humans live by images and visions. Given the pressures toward it, the pastor must often fight off an understanding of himself or herself as a competitive entrepreneur out to build a successful church. We are members of a team and members of a body, participants and servants with other clergy in the common mission to which God beckons all our congregations and their leaders. In their best moments, all true professional guilds have some sense of this kind of commonality and, ambiguously to be sure, they express that calling in their ethics of mutual concern and obligation.

Notes

1. Terrence J. Johnson, *Professions and Power* (London: Macmillan, 1972), p. 17.

2. Christian Church (Disciples of Christ), "My Ministerial Code of Ethics" (Indianapolis: Department of Ministry and Worship, 1968).

3. Office of the General Assembly, Presbyterian Church of the U.S.A. (*The Book of Order*, New York, 1967), sec. 51.03.

4. Joan Mabon, "My Friend, the Former Pastor . . ." *Alban Institute Newsletter* (April 1980). Reprinted by permission from *Action Information*, published by the Alban Institute, Inc., 4125 Nebraska Avenue, NW, Washington, DC, 20016. Copyright April 1980. All rights reserved.

5. Christian Church (Disciples of Christ), "My Code," p. 5.

6. *Baptism, Eucharist, and Ministry*, Faith and Order Paper No. 111, (Geneva: World Council of Churches, 1982), p. 4.

7. Ibid., p. 31.

8. Office of the General Assembly, *Book of Order*, sec. 57.043.

9. Gordon Kaufman, "Are Traditional Mennonite Approaches Adequate?" in Donald B. Kraybill and Phyllis Pellman Good, eds., *Perils of Professionalism: Essays on Christian Faith and Professionalism* (Scottdale, Pa.: Herald Press, 1982), p. 168.

10. Daniel J. Levinson, *The Seasons of a Man's Life* (New York: Ballantine Books, 1978), pp. 144-49.

8

COMMUNITY OUTREACH AND SOCIAL ACTION

Both the biblical tradition and the idea of a profession mandate our "public ministry." This emerging term points to the aspects of our work that are often labeled "prophetic," but it addresses today's actual pastoral office more comprehensively. The term *public ministry* reminds us that the pastor is beholden to far larger claims than the wishes of a particular congregation. The attorney is called ultimately to interpret jurisprudence as part of justice; the physician, individual treatment as part of enhancing a community's health. The minister is called to see congregation-building and pastoral caring within a controlling social vision that involves doing justice and loving mercy in faithfulness to God.

RECENT HISTORY

The 1960s saw a remarkable increase in public ministry. On the spur of the moment, local pastors packed their bags and left for Selma, or Washington, or Jackson, to participate in the Civil Rights movement. They meant to bring a witness of the church to the public order. Some sought approval of their congregational leaders, some did not. Not a few ended in jail and missed Sunday responsibilities back home.

Most of these pastors survived the friction their acts provoked. The social awareness of white churches grew by a quantum leap. Evangelism took on a new breadth as thousands of formerly disenchanted students and social dropouts took hold of an active, committed faith. Measurable social change toward justice was the result. Painful as were those years for many local churches, the '60s were far from the disaster some labeled them. They were a time of catching up on the prophetic side of witness.

A broad history of public ministry in these years would need to delve into the mid-century liberal churches' rootage in the earlier Social Gospel movement, but foremost was the role of the black churches and their preacher-martyr, Martin Luther King, Jr. From the time of the bus boycott in the mid-'50s to the time of his assassination in 1968, wrote Sidney Ahlstrom, Martin Luther King "did more to preserve the ethical dignity of the American people than any other person in the country."[1]

The antiwar movement inherited much of its verve and method from the Civil Rights marchers. Civil disobedience became more widespread, and more angry. Young men were dying in far off lands whose names to most Americans meant little but a challenge to our triumphalist assumptions. Those assumptions gradually eroded as television exposed the cruelties and atrocities and waste of war. Again the clergy were in the fray, and again on the basis not of congregational consensus but of individual conscience and professional autonomy.

Clergy in both the Civil Rights and the antiwar movements believed their actions were conscience-building for the community of faith. They were following a "profession" in the sense both of committed personal calling and of institutional obligation. Some clergy argued that their independent activism was superbly educational, for people were growing as they came to terms with their pastor's actions, *ex post facto*.[2] Others, more cautious, tried for congregational discussion in advance, or even carefully explained that their activism was on their free time, their days off. Virtually all churches had to take note of the public moral and religious issues because some clergy, even if not their own, were involved.

The legacy of the older Social Gospel movement and of the '60s can now be identified in highly diverse places: in affluent suburban churches that sponsor inner-city soup kitchens; in inner-city black churches that work closely with tax-supported Opportunities Industrialization Centers; in clusters of "new evangelicals" like the Sojourners community; in the Catholic Maryknoll order with its liberation-oriented publications and its missionaries up and down Latin America; in the growing sanctuary movement in both Protestant and Catholic parishes. Few responsible church leaders would be found opposing or ignoring the prophetic, public side to ministry.

That fact, however, does very little to clear up the considerable confusion around pastoral identity and obligation in regard to public policy, societal needs, and church social action. Paul Ramsey was one of the more thoughtful and influential ethicists questioning not so much the presumptions of individual pastors who cry out in the wilderness, but of church councils themselves. Who speaks for the church? he asked. Hundreds of less scholarly but equally concerned pastors and denominational leaders can be heard today berating the "World Council theology" with its liberationist analysis.[3]

The conservative religious elements gathered together in Jerry Falwell's "Moral Majority" organization of the early 1980s further illustrate the present-day confusion in the Christian community. On what they believe to be Christian grounds, these folk seemingly oppose the entire reformist platform of the "mainline" movements. At the same time they have reversed an older evangelical opposition to political social action by religious groups, bringing the "third force" of fundamentalist American Christianity into the limelight. Their strength only intensifies the still nagging questions of pastoral ethics in prophetic ministry.

Professional ethics is little but sounding brass and stuffy

etiquette if it is not grounded in a passion for the larger issues of justice. It is easy for very proper, even relatively fair-minded, people to be ethical within a small frame and yet fundamentally wrong or negligent in matters of social justice. One thinks of the younger Billy Graham, as a revivalist religious leader of the early '50s, tolerating segregated audiences and organizing anti-Catholic sentiments against the election of John Fitzgerald Kennedy, or of the portion of "mainline" church leadership that only in 1969 or 1970 came to see the fundamental wrongness of the American stance in Vietnam.

Ahlstrom's citation of King is useful in two ways. First, like Gandhi before him, King and the many clergy who followed his banner symbolized the culture-shaping potential of the ministry if it draws on deep streams of religious idealism rather than simply the accumulated resentments of the disinherited. King lifted up a vision of principled redemptive love far more profound than a mere desire to right past wrongs with whatever means might lie at hand. Second, King showed that the ethical role of Christians and their leaders, far from being a matter of a scrupulous seeing, hearing, and doing of no evil, has an outward purpose that will contribute to the "ethical dignity" of a culture.

If our professional ethics goals of honesty and respect and loyalty among clergy do not arise out of these principles, they are tinkling cymbals. Professional ethics too can have prophetic powers, and understand all mysteries and all knowledge and yet gain nothing, for lack of love (I Cor. 13:2).

DILEMMAS OF PUBLIC MINISTRY

Before attempting any pastoral ethics guidelines for this area of public ministry, we can suggest a few of its dimensions with brief vignettes.

A public-spirited minister discovers that a self-appointed action committee has evolved from a church Bible study group and is opposing American participation in the United

Nations because the UN "offers a platform for the Communists." The committee has written a letter to the local newspaper about its convictions, using the church's name in identifying its study group.

A concerned pastor spends an average of half a day a week for about two months, helping organize a church coalition for stronger social welfare programs in the state. An opposing group within the congregation begins attacking the minister as unethical; the pastor, they say, is using "church time" for partisan political activity.

A minister, concerned that one presidential candidate is significantly more likely than another to pursue serious-minded arms negotiations with the Soviet Union, urges people in one of her mid-October sermons to vote for the candidate she favors. When a layperson of an opposite political persuasion argues that the minister's actions were inappropriate, the pastor uses her denomination's peace resolutions to justify her sermon.

A pastor is invited to address a baccalaureate service for the local high school in a rural Bible-belt town. She recognizes the public, civic nature of the occasion, and the highly evangelical style of the older clergy who will participate. She also knows that there is at least one Jewish family represented in the small graduating class. She wonders what kind of preaching and praying is to be done in mixed religious milieus under public auspices. She opts for an Old Testament text, and she prays without invoking the name of Jesus. The Jewish parents are profoundly grateful.

A young mother considering an abortion comes to her pastor.[4] She has two children, and her husband is leaving her, asking for a divorce. The young pastor finds the woman to be ambivalent about the abortion. She has some moral reservations, difficult as it would be to have a child. The husband is altogether unsupportive, virtually out of the picture. In reporting the case, the pastor says he wants to avoid moralism. He counsels for a decision that would be best for the mother and the children, and refers her to a counselor "who would be better able to help her resolve her feelings."

As indicated by such instances as these, among the issues in pastoral ethics and public ministry are concerns for the autonomy of lay groups within a church, accountability for the pastor's energies and time, partisanship in prophetic action, sectarianism on occasions of public leadership, and moral clarity in the midst of pastoral care.

PUBLIC MINISTRY IMPERATIVES

One of the imperatives of public, prophetic ministry has already been introduced in chapter 4. We argued there that pastoral care carries a moral dimension. For their mental and spiritual health, people need to set their lives in a meaningful moral framework. Therefore the minister is called to reinforce, within and beyond the church, the moral environment in which we live. That means public ministry.

The last instance just above is a case in point. The minister apparently ignored the moral concern of the parishioner and treated her problem as one of emotional anxiety alone. That minister was not necessarily called on to impose a prochoice or prolife decision on the woman, or any stance in between. Ignoring the moral concern, however, misreads the woman's problem in at least some measure and belittles her human wholeness. It falls short of adequate pastoral care.

If religious faith and our own spiritual health involve a sense of the moral aspect of our lives, part of religious leadership involves attending to the contemporary moral environment. Clergy hardly have any exclusive assignment to attend to such public matters, but they are among those who are so charged. The idea that there is a dichotomy between pastoral nurture and prophetic, moral perspectives is mistaken.

Another imperative for public ministry is more commonly recognized: the biblical mandate for justice. This mandate is an inextricable part of God's self-disclosure in the scriptural record. Insight into God's ways with Israel and the creation arose out of the prophets' identifying with the poor and disenfranchised. Jesus ate with the publicans and sinners and preached blessedness to the poor as a sign of his own mission. Today's most visible inheritors of the prophetic and Social Gospel traditions argue in the same vein.

Looking at the social order from the standpoint of the voiceless and the poor is a rich and essential aspect of hermeneutic method. It is not that the church and its ordained ministry are the moral arbiters for the social order. It is not that we have or should have the power to force the world to "shape up" morally. Others share that vocation with us, Christian and non-Christian—people in government, business, labor, education, and other power centers. Nor do we of ourselves bring in the reign of God. That is God's to do. But in knowing God, and in trying faithfully to respond to God, we are thrown into the arena of public debate and public action. Judging by the whole of scripture, we can guess that God is less concerned for private pieties and "solemn assemblies" than with justice and mercy, particularly for the "least" (Matt. 25:40) in their suffering.

SOME AXIOMS AND OBLIGATIONS

Two procedural axioms can serve at this point. The two relate to each other in some tension. First, as we argued in chapter 3, the pulpit must be free. In no other way can the Spirit be free. Amos separated himself from the suspicion attached to professionalism by arguing that he was no prophet, nor a prophet's son. This freedom is assumed whenever a congregation engages a new pastor, but it often needs to be reiterated by the ministerial guild. It is as fundamental to our work as academic freedom is to the university faculty, even if not undergirded in our case by tenure. It is imperative lest interpreting scripture and the things of God be trammelled by convention and conformity, lacking that passionate engagement with the Word that takes place only in freedom.

In a superb little book, Walter Brueggemann says the pastor is called to a poetic task. The prophet exercises the prophetic imagination, he says, overcoming the numbness that inevitably accompanies a static, established order—what he calls the "royal consciousness." The prophet expresses an alternative consciousness, pointing to the possibilities of compassion for the dispossessed, to a new vision of justice. Imagination needs freedom.

Freedom always invites into a discussion its sibling concept, order. Even the creative artist, the poet, or the musician works with a highly disciplined, highly ordered skill. Freedom is not license. Therefore a second axiom must match the first: The pastor lives in a covenanted community with the congregation and the wider church. In exercising prophetic leadership, the minister works within a structure, in active dialogue with a community. That understanding of the arena for prophetic, public ministry needs emphasis, lest freedom dissolve into anarchy, callousness, or misanthropy.

This communal covenant includes the freedom, gives it a place, gives it substance. It also, however, disciplines the freedom. It asks that the freedom be used for opening the Word.

The pastor, then, weighs responsibilities of several sorts in considering prophetic witness. There is first of all the "near-neighbor" obligation, fulfilling the covenant with the congregation. That covenant means time for pastoral care, especially with the bereaved, the sick, and the troubled, as well as the pastoral care that is in prophetic teaching. In answering those who ask them how they can "get away with it," most activist pastors respond, "One earns this freedom through faithful pastoral care."

Second, there is faithfulness to the theological charter. Health is the ultimate mandate for the doctor; the whims of the hypochondriac are not. Likewise, one preaches and leads on the basis of a theological understanding of God's graced actions for justice, not on the whims of the political or ideological season. It is tempting, in the case of current social issues, to use the arguments at hand from persuasive editorialists and wise politicians, but the pastoral mandate and vision must have deeper rootage. The Enlightenment and secular philosophies of one sort and another are not enough.

We do not need to have ready answers for all human dilemmas. It is quite possible that there is a local issue on which there is "no word from the Lord," aroused as may be the local passions. There may be no moral choice, profound as the secular arguments for one side and the other may sound. On the highway, it is not more "right" to use the left-hand system as the British do, than the right-hand style, as Americans. Some issues are like that. In other matters, there may be a sound theological partisanship, but the minister may not yet have thought it through. There is nothing shameful in saying to the local reporter, "I haven't worked that out yet."

Third, the pastor will exercise due respect for the moral convictions and expertise of the laity. He or she is not an authority on all things political, economic, and social. The church is a corporate body, with its pastoral theologians as resources for the collective enterprise. Prophetic ministry cannot dictate to the people of the pew. Lay experience—in government, education, trade unions, business, social work—provides the data that must complement theological perspective if the church is to act and speak in the world.

A sound doctrine of the laity, then, undergirds the "freedom of the pew" for which we argued in chapter 3 as we discussed preaching. This line of reasoning allows for considerable disagreement within a single congregation, and within a denomination, as long as moral-theological discussions and social action are seriously and thoughtfully undertaken. In emphasizing the freedom of the pew, one congregation established a policy of "self-start social action." Any group of members was allowed to organize around a social or moral concern, and to use the church's name in public pronouncements and action as long as certain conditions were met: (1) The positions taken by the group were to be theologically based, with the religious ground carefully articulated. (2) Statements being issued had to report the size of the group, and the votes pro and con when there was not unanimity. The church's governing body agreed that funding for these groups could be appropriated even if two groups were advocating opposite positions on an issue. The goal was moral depth more than "right answers."

Fourth, there is a denominational claim on us. (There is also, let us hope, denominational support. It was a sad conclusion of a study of Little Rock pastors, during the 1950s racial crisis in the schools, that neither denominational nor ministerial peer group support was forthcoming for those ministers who risked their congregations' animus as they tried to interpret the needs for integration.)[5]

For a number of reasons, denominational pronouncements and policies are usually more progressive than would be a consensus of a local congregation.[6] They present one of the resources for a pastor for advocating social policy. This testimony from related Christians within the denominational family has a good chance of being taken seriously even by those who disagree. Even if the pastor disagrees with the denominational position, it can serve to introduce an issue that might otherwise have been passed by. The relative force of such pronouncements will differ among the traditions, of course. Moral persuasion is the primary force, however, even in the Roman Catholic tradition, where for example contraceptive practices supposedly banned by papal edict are practiced in good conscience by the majority of American Catholic couples. Private conscience has a standing in all traditions.

"Right answers" are less important in the church's public ministry than the simple imperative of introducing moral concern. The most destructive quality in social life is the one that isolates some arenas from moral consideration. During the early days of national anguish over Vietnam, the irresponsible pastors were not so much those who failed to oppose the war as those who, thinking to preserve harmony, helped or allowed their congregations to tiptoe around the issue altogether.

This moral force of denominational pronouncement can also be an ecumenical resource. One of the finest examples of assisting local congregations to practice their vocation as communities of moral discourse was found in 1983 as Protestant pastors led their congregations through the Catholic Bishops' letter on nuclear arms.

Finally, amorphous as it is, there is the claim of the disinherited themselves. They need food and health care and housing and education and justice. In nation after nation, they need access to the social and political structures of their societies. The pastor, like any other Christian, needs to see their poverty as a claim upon the neighbor-love of the Christian community. The priest and the Levite were professionals who passed by this need. Let the way we exercise professional leadership be different from that. The disenfranchised need to be in our prayers in liturgy, in our benevolence budgets, in our study of Christian social policy, and in our concerns when we act as Christian citizens and community organizers. "He has put down the mighty from their thrones, and exalted those of low degree" (Luke 1:52) sang Mary, and throughout the scriptures are echoes of her song of God's care for the outcast. Worshiping this God, we in our pastoral and congregational life will do the same.

Just as an ethical business manager weighs the interests of three sets of people who have a stake in the corporation—the stockholders, the employees, and the public at large—so the minister must weigh at least four claims: responsibilities to pastoral needs, to the theological charter, to moral consensus in the wider Christian community, and to the needs of the disenfranchised. Should the pastor march, write, picket, preach? There are no formulas. Different clergy will weigh the situation differently according to their positions in those categories outlined by Ralph Potter (see chapter 1). Much as they are all Christian pastors, they may nonetheless use different styles of moral reasoning, express different institutional loyalties and different theologies. They share, however, the common professional vocation of social engagement and public ministry.

Public trust. Opportunity for community leadership and public ministry comes about in part because of the multifaceted professional roles that clergy play. In spite of that, they are often ill-prepared for the mundane details of those responsibilities. As clergy take on public responsibilities, they need to learn the ways of the world lest they be taken in. Josh Davenport is a chaplain moving into a new community. Ted Jennings, a young local pastor, tells him of a house for sale at $64,000, the house of an elderly widow whom Jennings is helping with her affairs. The price is suggested by a realtor in Jennings' congregation, who is handling the details. The house is being sold because the widow is going into a church home. The life-care arrangement is one in which the home receives all her estate upon her admission. Jennings himself has power of attorney for the widow and will manage the sale of the home, with the help of the realtor.

Davenport discovers that the local housing market would easily make the house worth $100,000 or more. He discovers that the realtor had a "friend" who was buying the widow's house for $61,000, so Davenport offers the asking price immediately. The realtor, however, immediately closes with the "friend," shutting Davenport out. The realtor castigates Jennings for telling Davenport about the house at all.

Later Davenport and Jennings reflect on avarice and innocence. Jennings knew too little about real estate to check the values of property beyond the word of one realtor. He trusted his parishioner. He wonders if he had any business helping the widow in her affairs. Recognizing the "friend" as a front for the realtor himself, they wonder with each other whether to blow the whistle with the local board of realtors. Davenport feels a little guilty for having so relished the deal he had hoped to make that he didn't raise a question more promptly about the short-changing of the church home to which the money would go.

As the word leaks out, the names of both Jennings and his

parishioner suffer. Jennings resolves that he will learn more diligently the wisdom of serpents if he takes on a public trust like this again.

Time in community service. Our dedication to freedom of the pulpit does not release us from various aspects of our professional accountability vis-á-vis the employing congregation. One of these aspects is our use of time.

Clergy often have the competence and the freedom for considerable community service beyond the congregation. Public ministry can be a heady, satisfying experience. It can also be seductively self-important, to the extent of displacing laypersons who ought to be taking on public service while the clergy tend to their own work as coaches and theologians-in-residence, behind the scenes.

When community service begins to consume an unwarranted amount of the minister's time, therefore, it is wise to seek an evaluation from the parish leadership, lest self-deception rule the day and more urgent pastoral responsibilities be neglected. One congregation relieved a pastor of half his work load while he served as a reformist school board chairman in a major city. They confirmed the importance of his community service and arranged for lay and professional coverage for the administrative and pastoral tasks that he had to put aside for the time.

CHURCH AND STATE

Some professional ministerial guidelines in community outreach and social action derive from reflecting on the relations of church and state. Common ground for clergy among highly conservative evangelicals, activist ecumenical Protestants, and traditional Roman Catholics will be elusive, but some attempt at outlining this dimension of pastoral ethics is imperative.

Theologically understood, the church has a reality that transcends the boundaries of nation and the moralities of culture. At the same time, the church operates within contemporary secular democracies as one of the many voluntary agencies. This double viewpoint accounts for much of the confusion about issues of church and state. It also provides both the platform and the societal openness for social action by the churches. We do not suffer the kind of ban faced by the churches of the Soviet Union, where the state emasculates the conduct of religious pursuits by limiting religion to in-house, "spiritual" ceremonials and nurture. We are free to express in the public arena, in both word and deed, our moral and religious convictions.

We need not discuss further the theological imperatives that underlie church and clergy witness in the public square. As a discipline, pastoral ethics deals more particularly with appropriate ways to exert religious influence in the public arena.

Begin with the most notorious array of cases, those of civil disobedience, of law-breaking in the name of God. One pastor withholds all income tax as an act of conscientious protest against American militarism. Another offers "sanctuary" to an "illegal," a fearful political refugee from Central America. Another blocks traffic in front of an industrial plant that makes nuclear bombs.

We may venture one axiom as follows: Except in extreme cases the pastor may and should affirm the reality of order that the state provides. Disagree as we may with its racism, its militarism, its sexism, and its economic favoritism for the rich and powerful, the state and its role of governance is ordinarily valuable. Therefore, given the large amount of democratic flexibility afforded us on the American scene, even while engaging in civil disobedience that breaks statutory law, we do not intend to undermine the state. True *civil* disobedience seeks another end: consciousness-raising, education, the focusing of public concern on an issue, so that the society and the state may proceed with a better order.

It is inconsistent for the civilly disobedient, after breaking the law to make their point, to then flee arrest, jump bail, hide from the authorities, or harbor personal bitterness as the state proceeds with its vocation to order. Protesting arrest through the courts, on the other hand, affirms the state's order as well as continues one's advocacy.

Civil disobedience, then, is very different from revolution, justified in nonpacifist thought when nonviolent means are exhausted, when the majority are long oppressed by brutal tyranny, and when the costs of violence and the undermining of authority are seriously taken into the tragic calculus. Some legitimate actions hold elements of both civil disobedience and revolt. In the Philippines, Cardinal Jaime Sin called for persons by the tens of thousands to block the tanks of Ferdinand Marcos as they headed for Camp Crame. His was a revolutionary action against a particular state regime, but it was also highly affirmative of order and discipline.

Occasionally such activist clergy as those described above are accused of hating their country. Clearly, the concept of a higher loyalty curtails blind patriotic fervor for any thinking Christian. In a nation that itself interprets its own legitimacy not through brute force but through natural or divine law, social criticism and reformist—even civilly disobedient—action are thoroughly defensible by loyal citizens, activist clergy included.

Faithful prophetic action is not coercive. The police power belongs to the state. In medieval and modern instances when we of the church had the sword, our inquisitions corrupted the witness of the gospel, and we are well rid of it. We have shed those weapons, as David shed the armor of Saul, and we have found other instruments for our witness. As Bishop Tutu has said more than once in his courageous witness for the church, "There is no sword in the hand of David." The task of the prophet was not to wrestle the social order into conformity with his own vision; it was to lament the suffering of the disenfranchised by pointing to the justice of God, and to present a vision of righteous hope to the people.

PARTISAN POLITICS AND THE PASTOR

More commonplace questions of pastoral leadership also present themselves. How partisan should the pastor be? To speak in generalities that lack political implications is usually to leave the prophetic vision vacuous. Yet to take political sides seemingly reduces the church to something less than it is, to make it just one more pressure group among so many.

Both statements are facts of life. Therefore, both will help to guide the minister. Generally the minister should speak and act with issues in mind, not political candidates. Hunger, war, poverty, corruption, pollution, shoddy public education, the rape of the earth, vengeful prison systems, unsafe streets, drug addiction and drunkenness—these problems all lend themselves to prophetic study and preaching. Highlighting them is part of faithfulness to the task of exalting God and attempting the godly life in societal ways. There will often be times when such study and preaching seem to guide the voter one way or the other, but the concerns are urged by the church on both political parties, not one. There is no "Christian" party in American politics. We help sustain the unity of the nation and thereby foster greater justice by not creating one.

In one particularly passionate presidential election, a minister simply felt impelled to share his convictions, after long prayer and study, that he as a Christian should vote for one candidate in the name of peace. He had the grace then to step down from the pulpit and speak humbly and confessionally from the floor, at the same time inviting discussion after service. There was a great deal of integrity both in the speaking and in the stepping down. Pastoral ethics was well served.

Can the pastor run for office, or take an active part in politics? Style is part of the answer. The minister cannot, if his or her way of politicking is primarily to condemn the other side as evil, un-Christian, or vicious. A voice from South Africa speaks in the press: "Apartheid is not reformable. It is evil. You can't reform evil. You have to destroy it." True, if it could be done, but persons, even those involved in apartheid's enforcement, partake of both good and evil. We don't attack persons the same way we attack evil.

Both its "highly differentiated" view of pastoral ethics and the inevitable ambiguities of holding political power account for the Vatican's recent proscribing of all public office for its clergy. The priest in the Roman tradition is a person set further apart for churchly activity, as illustrated in some of the arguments for celibacy and priestly dress. There is not only the latent (and realistic) fear that energy will be drained from churchly service, but also that a kind of ascribed purity of motive and deed will be tainted in the knock-about of political service and action. Our position is less rigid. Although American Protestants cherish the traditions of church-state separation, a less highly differentiated view of pastoral ethics allows more readily for an occasional entry of clergypersons into appointive or electoral office, without demitting ministerial standing (see chapter 1).

Active political life is a right of everyone, and in our view the clergy have a right to spend their private time in such a pursuit just as others do. They can defend themselves as free citizens, and as conscientious ones. They also have a right to think of this exercise of civic freedom as an instructive enterprise for others who respect them to see, learn about, and possibly emulate.

At the same time, clergy will need to remember the blurring of that line between occupational and personal life that comes with being a professional. The professional's life and person are more available to the "client" than is the case with the technician and blue-collar worker. Therefore, that a partisan within the congregation, one on an opposing side, may take offense at the pastor's entering politics is to be expected. Working out the differences with that parishioner, however, can be a wholesome experience.

In several respects, clergy serve as "chaplains" not only in the military forces and hospitals but to the society at large. Clergy are invited to give baccalaureate addresses, to invoke God's blessing on various civic occasions, to offer grace at meals of the local chamber of commerce. In all of these circumstances, there is an element of "civil religion" for the minister to understand. Coming to terms with the exercise should not be allowed to destroy our critical distance. If that seems impossible, it is wisest simply to turn down the invitation. One's presence must not be allowed to imply undiscriminating approbation. One can attend labor conventions *and* the local manufacturer's association. I would not pray at a rally for the Ku Klux Klan!

There is a further matter of sensitivity. The minister at the baccalaureate service mentioned at the beginning of this chapter was right in her choice of text. Civic occasions demand allowing for the integrity of non-Christians in the audience. Denominational partisanship has no place in the Memorial Day prayer.

CORPORATE CHURCH AND INDIVIDUAL PASTOR

As pastor, expressing prophetic leadership is shot through with what the cynic from outside easily labels compromise. The purist argues that the minister is not called on to be successful but to be faithful, and asks adamantly to hear clarion calls for disarmament, for curbing the power of transnational corporations, for stopping the foreclosures of family farms. The thinking pastor responds by answering that the issues are never so simple, that the minister's call is theologically grounded prophecy and not simplistic politicking, and that faithfulness itself has many dimensions. One of those dimensions is concern for the unity of the congregation.

Pastoral ethics does not sell out by backing away from controversy. Most churches concerned for more than trivial matters will encounter disagreement over the implications of Christian faith for social policy time and time again. The pastor, however, has a far broader mandate than to think through his or her own position in these matters and then serve them up to the congregation. That mandate is to nurture the growth of a congregation—growth in faith, in cohesive morale, and in depth of prophetic witness too.

There are many times when the teacher should keep private opinion close to the chest while the classroom debates and studies. That is not compromise. That is good teaching. So too for the pastor.

One reason ministers must be slow to judge one another goes far beyond good etiquette and loyalty within the guild. It is because we do not know from outside what the pressures and needs inside another congregation may be. Picketing and provocative pronouncements may seem a faithful response to the gospel mandates for one, while quiet behind-the-scenes teaching and pastoral prodding appear the same for another. We can ask that the leadership of every priest and minister give witness and active nudging concern toward God's shalom. If we care about the church, we dare not self-righteously ask that all faithfulness take the same form.

Notes

1. H. Richard Niebuhr and Daniel D. Williams, eds., *The Ministry in Historical Perspectives* (San Francisco: Harper & Row, Publishers, 1983), p. 296.

2. Harold R. Fray, Jr., *Conflict and Change in the Church* (Boston: Pilgrim Press, 1969), pp. 21-22.

3. Paul Ramsey, *Who Speaks for the Church?* (Nashville/New York: Abingdon Press, 1967).

4. Earle E. Shelp and Ronald H. Sunderland, eds., *The Pastor as Prophet* (New York: Pilgrim Press, 1985), p. 45.

5. Ernest Q. Campbell and Thomas F. Pettigrew, *Christians in Racial Crisis* (Washington, D.C.: Public Affairs Press, 1959), pp. 88-91.

6. Jeffrey Hadden, *The Gathering Storm in the Churches* (Garden City, N.Y.: Doubleday & Co., 1969), ch. 5.

9

PUBLIC RELATIONS, EVANGELISM, AND CHURCH GROWTH

The gospel moves us to announce the Good News of God. Church folk give "testimony"; they rehearse their faith and celebrate their saving experience. As a now commonplace but profound assertion has it, we speak as beggars, telling other beggars where we have found bread. We sing, as do the psalms. We "boast" as Paul says of himself. We don't keep it all to ourselves.

The gospel also instructs us to evangelize, to make the announcement. It gives us the Great Commission. Paul finds testimony an inescapable part of his own faith. "For necessity is laid upon me. Woe to me if I do not preach the gospel" (I Cor. 9:16). "Always be prepared," says Peter, " . . . to account for the hope that is in you" (I Pet. 3:15).

The ethics of evangelism, then, begins with this testifying-and-being-sent stance. Part of our most fundamental obligation is to increase faith among near neighbors and far neighbors. A pastoral ethics annual checkup may well begin with the question, Do you yearn that people believe?

The issues of ministry ethics begin to compound immediately, however, once we take a pulse that way. Evangelism has come to mean something far more specific than expressing that yearning appropriately. It means accessions to church membership and the processes that lead to that. It means "decisions for Christ" at the revival meeting. It means public relations and radio programs and newspaper copy. How much any one of these transactions correlates with growth in loyalty, joy, and obedience to the God we know in Jesus Christ is a matter of some question. Some ministers appear to perform well in such matters, but with questionable motives. Some yearn all right, but being fearful of duplicity in motive, they back away from these or any steps that might actually expedite the expansion of Christianity.

FOUR AFFIRMATIONS

We may achieve some clarity by means of four affirmations. Then, later in this chapter, we can look at method in both evangelism and public relations more explicitly.

(1) The goal of evangelism—increase in faith—is not to be confused with means. Swelling church membership, larger crowds at church, or increased "religious" programming on the media may or may not mean successful evangelism in the more profound sense. Ultimately God is the judge, and in the judgments we make, make them as we must in our leadership roles, we must always remember that. It is not at all unusual that material gains of this sort make for cheapening of faith and shallower spirituality.

(2) Persons are ends, not means. The chief temptation in evangelism is using persons for self-aggrandizement. In the most blatant form, we point to revivalists who boast of "winning" souls for Christ, but churches on Main Street glow with pride in just the same way when their institution succeeds, new members join up, or the steeple is higher than the next one on the block. Motives are never pure, and celebrating good signs can mean either rejoicing in the proper realities or pride in the wrong ones; the easy confusion of one for the other is regularly on the mind of the ethicist.

Persons are ends, not means. Struggling church boards have been heard to say, "We need new members to help us pay the bills." In *With Faith and Fury*, an *Elmer Gantry* of the 1980s, Delos Banning McKown writes of his protagonist,

> The harder he had to work for each new convert, the more important each potential convert became. The more important each potential convert became, the more devastating the loss Manly felt over each one who had "rejected Jesus," as he liked to put it, but had, in fact, merely deluded him. Although he did not recognize it, his evangelism became less the doing of the Lord's will and more the doing of his own will.[1]

The temptation to succumb at least in part to Manly's attitude plagues us all. Most of us come out with a more healthy position, inviting new members without a hard sell. The low-key minister who *never* asked anyone to be a member in the church he served, believing that faithful service would simply move people in due time, had an enviable integrity too.

(3) In personal evangelism, our goal is a person's ultimate well-being; in the culture, shalom. Nowhere does theological disposition more profoundly color pastoral work than at this very point. "Ultimate well-being" begs many questions. One person may believe in a literal hell and a God who judges according to verbal assent to brittle definitions of orthodoxy. In that case "ultimate well-being" might justify action that a more charitable doctrine and more open pastor would dismiss as outright wrongdoing. If we believe that God asks of the church a concern for the society rather than a sectarian withdrawal from it, evangelism justifies—and demands— that we pursue social action and a use of the arts in ways that would be alien to sectarian strategies.

Pastoral ethics can attempt to understand the continuum along which different clergy stand in these matters, but one's own stance must be taken. Thoughtful pastoral action, I would argue, affirms both the free autonomy of the person and the need for conversion toward obedience in Christ. The paradox is as old as Abraham, but it will not go away. It means that we do not manipulate people into believing, although we continue with the invitation into servanthood.

Christians believe that the self-sufficient, psychological "autonomy" supported by a secular world view will ultimately fall short of that well-being we know in faith. Coercion, however, contradicts the conviction; it distorts rather than nourishes faith.

Similarly, the institutional church is a vehicle toward the ends of God. Forcing conformity to the church's norms, however, or making membership in the church the chief end for our service and witness in the world prostitutes the mission of the church itself. Church growth is important, but evangelism has a broader content.

(4) Evangelism must go hand in hand with witness for justice. It is not too strong to assert that the alternative is easily a kind of heresy or blasphemy—presenting to the world an imaginary god, a god who is not God. Christ stands in the prophetic line (Luke 4:16-21), and the God we know in Christ is skeptical of "solemn assemblies" (Amos 5:21) and of those who merely say "Lord, Lord" (Matt. 7:21). Inviting people to encounter a Christ who lacks that dimension, whose church lacks it, is not evangelism.

James Cone wrote about trying in his younger days to help white people understand the injustice they inflicted on blacks even though they claimed loyalty to Jesus. After an encounter on a bus, he said to a white woman, " 'Madam, you look like a Christian. . . . How could you say the things you said to me when Jesus said what you do to the least you do to him?' 'You are not Jesus,' she replied with hate and violence in her eyes. 'Get the hell out of my face, you nigger!' I began to realize," says Cone, "that even if people know the truth, they will not necessarily do it. . . . [R]eligion did not automatically make people sensitive to human pain and suffering. Perhaps black people were right. What white people needed was a conversion experience."[2]

The word is well chosen. Conversion, *metanoia*, means turning toward God. If the evangelical dimension of the pastor and the congregation presents only a sentimental Jesus or a wishy-washy God, who is not the One concerned for the least, the ethics of evangelism is also violated.

PROFESSIONAL PERSPECTIVE

Certain dimensions of professional ethics also contribute to our self-understanding as evangelists. The professional has a calling that transcends loyalty to employer and client. As professional, the pastor is not simply an employee of the congregation, at its beck and call. Theologically, the call to ministry is from God, confirmed by the church. (Even the Internal Revenue Service says the minister is "self-employed.")

The minister serves according to criteria well beyond the direction and the material compensation by the "client." "A profession," says the Medical Association code, "has for its prime object the service it can render to humanity; reward and financial gain should be a subordinate consideration." "Humanity" is far broader than a specific, paying clientele!

In noting the same breadth of obligation, Joseph Fichter, who pioneered in using the sociology of occupations for understanding religious professionals, said this of the Catholic priest: "His pastoral and fatherly role is focused directly on his own parishioners, but his missionary role reaches out to all souls, regardless of their religious and denominational affiliation."[3]

These are idealistic sentiments, of course. Nonetheless, the minister who lacks the missionary sense, the desire to go beyond the "technician's" role that would merely serve the congregation's institutional efficiency, falls short of the best definition of his or her work. The church, to use one model from Avery Dulles' *Models of the Church*, is called to be *herald* as well as institution.[4] The pastor is evangelist as well as institutional enabler. From such duality comes the ethical quandary we have already encountered more than once: How much does the pastor "owe" to the congregation, how much to the unlimited pastoral needs of the community at large, to people outside the membership?

Ostensibly, the minister's primary "client" is the congregation; theologically however, the goal of the congregation is not self-aggrandizement but service to the world. Institutional success is important only to the degree that it serves the needs of the world to grow in loving God and loving neighbor.

We may now propose a conceptual framework for the minister's work with people outside the congregation. That work is (1) direct care, love of neighbor; (2) theological outreach for Christian faith; and (3) leadership for the congregation's own self-understanding.

(1) The pastor is seen by many outside the church as a professional whose services can be engaged like those of a lawyer or architect. People come for counsel, for weddings, for funerals. The minister will decide how much time to invest in positive responses to these requests. The important concern at this point is self-critical insight in these encounters. The goal is to increase faith. Always seeing "potential new member" written large behind each of these contacts distorts pastoral care, important as finding a spiritual home or learning disciplined worship may be for many of these outsiders.

(2) A secondary goal beyond service to these "outsiders," then, is theological outreach for Christian faith. If as we believe, the lone Christian is virtually a contradiction in terms and life in the church part of the full Christian discipleship and not just a means to private spiritual well-being, interpreting the Christian message to outsiders comes to be part of pastoral obligation.

In this assignment, inappropriate appeals are all too easy. Fear, for example. ("Where will your soul be if you die tomorrow?") Or loneliness. (An old Stan Frieberg religious spot commercial: "Doesn't it get a little lonely out on that limb, without him?"[5]) Family unity. ("The family that prays together stays together.") Emotional security, and so on.

Working with a person's emotions and anxieties is often part of theologically sound evangelism. It can also be dishonest manipulation. In spite of assertions and assumptions in upbeat advertisements of the religious life, a person may be made *more* lonely by professing faith in Jesus Christ (cf. Matt. 10:35, "against . . . father, . . . mother"), *less* successful in business, considerably troubled by the cares and injustices of the world, even "persecuted for righteousness' sake."

(3) Evangelism and promotion by the pastor should have an educative aspect. We go about them as provocateurs—intent not only on serving others or on helping them encounter Christ but also on serving the congregation's vision. We are not hired to evangelize while excluding the congregation from evangelizing. We do our best work when we inspire and nurture the laity in their work of outreach in the name of God.

METHOD IN EVANGELISM AND PROMOTION

In a culture like ours, evangelism takes many material forms: coffee-break discussions of personal faith, "Come-with-me-to-church" invitations to friends, organized encounters between visitors and newcomers to a neighborhood, revivals and preaching missions, media events, newspaper advertisements, financial campaigns.

The task for pastoral ethics is to sort out the strategies that are appropriate to ministry. The consequentialist in ethics may argue that any method is legitimate as long as a good end is served. The means, however, is virtually a part of the end. The medium is part of the message. The "anything goes" approach is self-defeating, especially when the "product" is a matter of faith and integrity itself.

We might propose some rules for ethical evangelism and promotion, but rules too easily handicap us with their lifelessness. The broader, richer language of appropriateness seems best. What is appropriate, what is fitting in the evangelistic outreach of the church? Some examples of what is *not* appropriate follow.

One television evangelist interrupted his hour-long program seven times to offer as many different gifts and trinkets to viewers who would phone or write in with their names and addresses. He also interrupted the program an equal number of times with urgent appeals for funds. Most of the money would go to support that very program.

We believe the church should grow. One of the principles of the "church growth movement" is the targeting of homogeneous population groups for new churches and for the revival of old ones. Church people of a feather flock well together. The amazing story of Pentecost with its anti-Babel implications, and the ministry of reconciliation between "Jew and Greek, slave and free" are left to one side.

A brash new young assistant minister announces her intention to get something about the church into the paper every week of the first year she is on the job. She nearly succeeds, but at the cost of some stretching of the truth about the newsworthiness, quality, and scope of congregational activities.

A hyped-up evangelism program involves training neighborhood visitors in methods best described as hard-sell. The trainers reflect a manipulative kind of regard for "prospects," as they call them, and an attitude of certainty about their own formulas for belief, insisting that no alternative avenues into Christian faith have any merit.

A church fund-raiser says his first principle is never to identify personally with the situation of the pastor or congregational leaders he is training. Feeling their stresses, he says, would cut into his effectiveness in manipulating the fund-raising drive as a whole.[6]

PRINCIPLES OF ACTION

Public relations and marketing materials reek of manipulative approaches to other persons. In them the subtle line between persuasion and psychological coercion is crossed repeatedly. No one who attempts to reach out to the public can avoid meeting that boundary, of course. Some will define a breach of ethics far more conservatively than others. Nonetheless, attempting some guiding principles is imperative. The following suggest themselves:

(1) Cherish and respect the person or the public being addressed. Again, persons are not means. Advertising, public relations, and evangelism for Christian faith cannot appropriately demean persons, treating them like objects instead of the subjects they are. Evangelism that begins with listening, as good counseling does, that truly hears persons in their life situations, will find the contagion of faith made possible. (*Communicate* is too shallow a word for the process.) Brainwashing, cultism, and exploitation are but the end of the trail that forgets this principle.

(2) Inform, do not propagandize. Sales efforts and advertising for commercial products have the legitimate role of informing the public of available goods and services. Misrepresentation in advertising, for the sake of extracting money and loyalty from the naive and gullible, rightly angers us. So does it also in local church newsletters and denominational magazines. Good writing doesn't need false hyperbole.

(3) Share. A whole series of words and images guides us in evangelizing and promoting. These are honest words, which do not coerce or manipulate. *Testimony* is one. We "confess" faith. We keep a lamp from being hid beneath a basket. Witness of this sort speaks in the first person indicative, not the second person imperative. "I have found that such and such"; "I felt as if God had so and so"; "I believe this and this."

Christian teaching that has integrity is invitational, not imperious. It experiences and inquires after truth and bids others come along to see for themselves. Philip says to Nathanael, "Come and see," echoing a theme that runs through a whole section of the first chapter of John. Pastoral ethics helps us with the theology of missions.

(4) Maintain integrity, even when it makes places rough that smooth, duplicitous talk could lubricate. Hiding the demands of faith "till later" is counterproductive.

(5) Avoid the worship of numbers. Other norms guide virtuous church promotion. Growth best comes incidentally, as faith is celebrated and shared. Or it does not come; the

gospel can be an offense. Testing all things by numbers makes for misrepresentation; it easily skews evangelism by causing it to avoid the offense.

(6) Be efficient; it is good stewardship. Now, after these other concerns have been affirmed, we acknowledge and follow many of the "how-to" materials in public relations resource books and evangelism workshops. Sending out mass mailings while ignoring the Sunday morning visitor from the neighborhood is bad stewardship. The visitor is far more likely to be asking for help or to be considering service in a community of faith. By contrast, the expensive mass mailing usually falls on deaf ears.

(7) Make "inclusiveness" an affirmative action. With this principle, we come full circle to the original imperative of evangelism. All too many congregations and pastors believe they welcome the stranger, and yet they do nothing to let the stranger feel welcomed. Such passive openness is more likely to prevent growth than the scandal of believing. It is also likely to deprive a congregation of the lively chemistry of diverse members with their diverse gifts. It deserts the mission of God on earth.

Notes

1. Delos Banning McKown, *With Faith and Fury* (Buffalo: Prometheus Books, 1985), p. 231.

2. James H. Cone, *My Soul Looks Back* (Nashville: Abingdon, 1982), p. 26.

3. Joseph H. Fichter, *Priest and People* (New York: Sheed and Ward, 1965), p. 3.

4. Avery Dulles, *Models of the Church* (Garden City, N.Y.: Doubleday & Co., 1974).

5. James Gustafson in Thompson, *Stewardship*, p. 162.

6. Ibid., p. 153.

10.

PERSONAL LIFE

Virtuous professional performance grows from deeper roots than professional codes and rules, helpful as such guidelines may be. The true source of good ministry is found in our fundamental orientation toward the work and toward the world, in our inner dispositions and attitudes. From these flow initiative and energy, our ability for self-management, our patience and, God willing, some degree of wisdom. Such qualities can be barely hinted at in professional canons of ethics. An essay on pastoral ethics ultimately moves, therefore, to such varied subject matter as ascetic theology, personal faith, and personal lifestyle.

The word *orientation* means a response to a point on the compass. Likewise ministerial disposition and attitudes of the self come about as response to reality outside ourselves. They depend on our perceptions of that reality. The Christian's disposition toward the world is shaped as response to God.

Ministry has as one of its chief tools not a spectroscope or lathe or even a Bible and the church building, but the human self. Pastoral ethics involves attention to the mental and spiritual health of the self.

FREEDOM OF SELF: THE PUBLIC-PRIVATE BOUNDARY

Jim Rockway went the usual route into ministry for his denomination. He attended its fine church-related college and then its leading seminary. He built an outstanding record in both places. He then moved right into position as associate minister with one of the princes of the pulpit, a man known across the region for the strong congregation he had built up. The church seemed full of community leaders in a city clustered around strong educational and governmental institutions.

From there, five years later, Jim Rockway moved to his own congregation, one with a similar constituency. In that parish, Jim's own record matched that of his first senior minister colleague. The next step, after eight years, was onto a seminary faculty. After only six months in that position, Jim said to an old friend he met at a conference: "Finally I feel free! All those years in the parish I was on display—couldn't dress the way I wanted, say the things I wanted, teach the things I wanted. I couldn't be myself."

Jim Rockway's name, if we focus on the sense of personal entrapment, is legion. For him, what ought to be among the most freeing and creative of vocations proved to be full of frustrating constraints.

One of the important elements in pastoral ethics may be labeled "freedom of self." Because personal integrity so undergirds professional life, in that life the public and private spheres coalesce more thoroughly than in blue-collar work or the work of a technician. The job cannot be left behind so easily at five in the afternoon. With all the room for unfairly exploiting professional authority at others' expense, it raises profound moral ambiguities. The professional position is more exposed to public view; privacy is not the same. The "publics" and institutional accountabilities are more numerous and diverse. Often there seem to be too many bosses, intruding even into private life.

Jim Rockway, of course, may simply have been too much of an antenna person, judging his own self-presentation in the world by the opinions of others, too little by his own inner compass.[1] "Doesn't other-directedness come with the territory?" someone may ask. "Don't ministers have to be extroverts?" Only to some extent. Jim Rockway felt that professional life constantly involved accommodating his own whims, temperament, *and* better judgments to the will and willfulness of the congregation, denominational authorities, and "Christian" niceties. After all, when frustrated, he couldn't relieve himself in public by venting his anger at the church leaders he was dealing with. His life seemed not his own.

It will help the Jim Rockways to conceive of professional responsibility as involving two concerns. Inevitably, as part of professional work in upbuilding human community, there come the kinds of restraints cataloged above. On the other hand, however, there is the necessity of attending to countervailing habits of heart and personal style, those that will counteract the potential destructive results of such other-directed restraints.

Important among those habits is the kind of personal strength and freedom that, without rancor, can engage others openly and clearly, even those who seem judgmental and negative. This kind of engagement reduces hidden agendas to a minimum. It informs people when communication seems difficult. It admits anger. It helps others in the congregation track the ups and downs of interpersonal and intergroup relationship.

The responsibilities of preaching and teaching with integrity have already been listed (chapter 3). That professional norm was compromised by Jim Rockway too often for his own good, much as he thought he was serving others and helping himself by being so accommodating. Jim also blunted the prophetic edge of his preaching, and the life of his congregations was shallower as a result. Jim simply didn't feel free to tell people what he thought, what he felt.

There is a deeper dimension to this freedom. Trusted for so many judgments, the professional easily errs by thinking of himself or herself too highly. When the reality fails to match the self-image, dissimulation sets in, and we pretend to be better than we are. Self-imposed inauthenticity begins to gnaw at our sense of freedom and wholeness. In the church the conception of ordained minister as spiritual or moral example reinforces this very natural human propensity. It becomes more and more difficult to admit to others our own foibles and frailty. We take ourselves too seriously; we lose all sense of humor about ourselves. That too may be part of Jim Rockway's problem. He may have cherished the pedestal on which people had placed him.

We ask of every professional an accurate reading of self-competence, so that referrals are appropriately made, for example, and so that interpersonal pretense is kept minimal. When one person admits vulnerability and limitation to another, the pastor included, openness and mutuality ensue. When the pastor comes down from the pedestal of self-importance, to serve and care, ministry begins.

CONGRUENCE

Or consider the case of Phil Greenfield.[2] Phil's poor understanding of private-public congruence for the professional cost him his job. At thirty-two, Phil Greenfield was an assistant minister at New Falls Church. He was commuting from a town about forty miles away during his first year's contract with this suburban church. Earlier, he had been divorced while leading a parish, had dropped out of ministry for secular work, and had then gravitated back to the church with some excitement when this opportunity had come.

Phil was getting over the hurts of the divorce, and he was living with a woman whom he hoped soon to marry. One major part of his portfolio included youth ministry. When gossip about Phil's living arrangements proved well-founded, and when parents of teenagers in the congregation discussed the matter in their board meeting, Phil's plea that his private life was his own did not save his job.

Obviously many people, some Christians included, do not adhere to or even believe in the traditional ideals that limit sexual cohabitation to official, documented marriage. And many of the arguments of contemporary Christian ethics persuasively temper rigid, "act-oriented" approaches to a sexual ethic. Nonetheless, for good reasons as well as weak ones, the traditional ideal is still the norm for most of the Christian community. It is not therefore surprising that Phil Greenfield should find himself in trouble.

Without discussion to the contrary, when it engages Phil Greenfield, the congregation assumes he adheres to a commonly held norm, even one that is breached time and time again in the community around New Falls Church and even within the congregation. There is an assumption that Phil Greenfield holds the views of his denomination, at least until he explains otherwise, his divorce notwithstanding.

The issue in Phil Greenfield's case is that of congruence. Especially in ministry, assuming that work and private life can be separated in the same way they can for the technician is erroneous. The professional is assumed to mean and to be committed to what he or she represents. This kind of integrity in professional life is well illustrated by the druggist who defined his work-world goals as the enhancement of human health. Becoming convinced of the carcinogenic potentials of smoking, he destroyed his $1,500 inventory of cigarettes and refused to sell them any longer, a loss in his case of about $1,200 monthly. If New Falls had worked out a more "contextual" sex and marriage ethic, or even if it were to attempt it around the occasion of Phil's contract renewal, congruence might be reestablished for his professional life in the New Falls congregation. Lacking that, Phil's living arrangements cannot be exclusively his private business; he is a teacher-pastor dealing in part of his work with a community's collective and intentional views on marriage and the family. Were he a technician, those arrangements could simply be his own.

TIME FOR WORK AND FAMILY

Accountability and diligence. One pastor, asked about issues in clergy ethics, began with an angry comment:

First, I would name laziness. The worst cheating is with time—at least I think it was for my predecessor. He made furniture and raised tropical fish with most of his energy, I think, right here in the parsonage, heavily consuming electrical power and his own time in the process. The utility bills must have been a third again what they should have been, paid for by the congregation. The man sang in a chorus and went to all the plays and concerts in the city. He took—and used!—subscription sermons. I think the reason he wouldn't let the parish build an office over in the church is fear that people would discover how rarely he would be there.

The ministry is one of the less structured of the professions. One priest said he was accountable for about twenty hours a week; the rest of the time was completely his own to schedule or waste. Another pastor, unable to use that kind of freedom creatively and proactively, conscientiously waited in his office with the complaint, "People never seem to call. I just sit here, and no one comes!"

This kind of problem is rare. Committed, well-trained, and imaginative pastors do not turn into "rectory priests," out of touch with their congregations. They are at work on the intellectual tasks of ministry or out with their people, either in pastoral care or in nurturing programs of mission as their time and energy allow. Nonetheless, some clergy need the old reminder about a fair day's work.

The more commonplace clergy problem involves ineptitude in managing time. This kind of failure disrupts both family obligations and spiritual wholeness. Another of our clergy diseases takes the form of complaint about impossible schedules and the burdens of overwork. We hear too often the confession-boast, "I don't take a day off." This clergy game is competitive on the surface, but underneath it also smacks of works righteousness and compulsive workaholism.

Professional accountability, once a pastor is engaged by a congregation, involves responsible schedule-keeping conscience, but not, for most at least, a no-days-off compulsiveness. We are to build a rhythm that integrates our lives through our work and our leisure, through attending to both professional service and personal wholeness. Sooner or later, burnout is likely to be the alternative.

Family life and leisure. Difficulties in family life for the clergy and other professionals have reached crisis proportions because of irreversible changes. The older pattern in which a male breadwinner was backed by a homemaker spouse is fast waning. Thousands of new double-occupation couples enter the American work force annually, among them those in which one partner seeks ordination and the other a separate career. Children are anticipated, but no permanent disruption of the two-track pattern. Moreover, the two-parent household is no longer even so thoroughly typical. Single-parent households proliferate through divorce. Given these changes, and given children, the seventy-hour and eighty-hour workweeks of a former generation of pastors are questionable even on moral grounds.

We interpret both ministry and marriage as covenants. Neither is merely a contract with the conditional commitment implied by that legal term. "Forsaking all others," we say in marriage, "I take you . . . for better, for worse, in sickness and in health, to love and to cherish" for our lifetimes. Such love in marriage demands time and care considerably beyond a Dagwood-to-Blondie peck on the cheek between church meetings and pastoral appointments. Likewise, the ordinand vows to be "a faithful priest to all [he or she] . . . is called to serve" and to persevere in building up the family of God. Both vows have an ultimate and all-consuming ring to them, as if nothing should intervene. Without a larger setting, as they compete with each other the two covenants will present insoluble dilemmas.

Christian faith, of course, provides just such a setting. Each vow is given to God. Faithfulness to God is the goal, not the merely horizontal obligation to church institution or human relationship. Given that answer, the inevitable competition between the two human covenants lends itself to less painful resolution. In the tension, we are to seek service to God. As one Anglican friend of mine put it in speaking of marriage and of ordination, "Two sacraments cannot conflict!" The vows are subordinate expressions of that single vocation: serving God.

Most clergy confront peculiar difficulties in these respects. As a class, we tend to set goals far beyond what we can realistically achieve. Our ambition is both for self and for God, but the first is often rationalized as the latter. Time for family life is eclipsed, the marriage vows nearly forgotten. We find the parish work so rewarding that we believe the extra ten hours a week are indispensable for the Spirit. We enjoy, even subtly foster, the dependency of others on us. As if the grace of God were not enough, we crave as well the commendations "We have such a tireless, dedicated pastor."

Meanwhile the spouse is caught in a peculiar bind. How can one fight a "holy" loyalty? A young wife may ask herself guiltily, Am I trying to keep him away from God's work by asking for a little time at home? A young husband wonders jealously whether the overextended clerical wife cares more for old men in the nursing home than for his own needs of intimacy.

We hear of the executive who is "married" to the corporation. The minister too can be married to the church—idolatrously and harmfully. If we ourselves criticize business people who shortchange their families because they make a false god of profit, we need to see the ambiguity in our own drive for institutional success as well. Both zeal for the Lord *and* competitive instinct panting after worldly success of one sort and another drive us toward our frenetic involvements.

Moral reflection on the family covenant, therefore, suggests a responsible but not an idolatrous commitment to the call into service of the church. It suggests realism about our vocation. Like YMCA workers, we spend great amounts of time with people in their leisure time, necessitating skewed schedules. We visit and have pastoral appointments in the weekend and evening periods that many other work groups usually have free for themselves. By way of balance and health, therefore, clergy patterns of a weekday off and blocks of daytime free make eminent good sense. The pattern needs to be interpreted to, or negotiated with, the congregation's leadership.

Furniture-building and tropical fish have their place as well! Hobbies make for mental health. Many a minister finds that in the tangible accomplishments of cooking, sewing, carpentry, painting, tennis, or music there is something so different from the amorphous and often frustrating task of working with people that the hobby is the therapy.

Good friends and a social life likewise promote health. They may be found within the parish, as was said earlier, as long as one recognizes the interference this may cause with the pastoral role. We have not urged a highly differentiated ethic for the clergy.

Indeed, the argument against close friends within the parish stems from an over-professional view of pastoral work. In a sense we carry on ministry by friendship—by doing together what good friends do—working, planning, playing, praying, grieving, worshiping. To extract ourselves from that is to advocate a kind of docetic doctrine of ministry, pulled back from material reality, sterile and formal.

The gift is to see everyone, if it may be said this way, as both parishioner and at least potential friend. Professional responsibility involves cultivating wisdom enough to know that friends can disagree, and integrity enough to separate roles when necessary. The newspapers recount daily the ways people in public office offer their friends favors that seriously violate the public trust and professional obligation. But friends within the congregation? Yes!

"DISTANCE" AND AVAILABILITY

Arguments of the sort just concluded easily appear to fly in the face of the often heard guideline of "professional distance" already cited in chapter 4. The term points us to the need for objectivity, lest we lose sight of certain boundaries. The boundaries are both those of role and of our own selfhood in intimate personal counseling. Losing sight of the boundaries, we lose the kind of objectivity that it is ours to offer. We become friend when the somewhat different gift of a strong mentor is needed, mere echo when true pitch or improved timbre is sought by the learning musician, co-fatalist when hope could be honestly offered, accommodating buddy when tough love is called for.

Professional distance also protects the self from exhausted burnout. The nurse and doctor simply cannot grieve as if losing a sibling or a spouse or a parent every time a patient dies, not if they are still to be available the next day for professional service. Moreover, while in the operating theater, the heart surgeon will do a better job by seeing the matter at hand as technical challenge rather than family crisis with enormous emotional weights in the balance for a potential widow. Surgeons do not operate on their own kin.

All that having been said, however, professional distance is not to become an excuse for emotional unavailability. Within reasonable and realistic limits, the person—the emotional and faithful selfhood—of the pastor is to be present in pastoral conversation and group leadership and the large-group teaching-preaching encounters of proclamation. Deadened, stiff, formal encounters should be as limited as possible, given the church's goals of care and faith. It is difficult to imagine that kind of relationship in any of the hundreds of human encounters reported in the New Testament.

PROFESSIONAL GROWTH

One of the most common professional requirements in the codes is maintenance of professional competence. "I will strive to grow in my work through comprehensive reading and careful study and by attending . . . conferences."[3] Because of the nature of the minister's work, there are two dimensions of the pastor's life that flow from this "professional" obligation: the need for technical competence and the need for mental and spiritual health. The latter concern figures prominently in the codes also: "I will cultivate my devotional life, continuing steadfastly in reading the Bible, meditation and prayer."

That study and reflection are professional obligations for the clergy may be best emphasized, perhaps, through analogy. People do not want the physicians who care for their health to be inept, out-of-date, unaware of available remedies for their ailments, or burned out. People do not want their lawyers to be out of touch with the law or unable to argue a case. Steady competence is incumbent on the doctor and the attorney.

Clergy competence is a matter more wide-ranging, but it entails the same kind of alertness to opportunities for continuing study and learning. Theology and the arts of pastoral care do not change with momentary scientific discoveries or new legislation and adjudication by the courts. Indeed, the momentary is often simply the faddish. It is the long Christian tradition against which we should test our teaching, and it is an ancient book we should present as plumbline and foundation for right building in the present. But inasmuch as we must therefore know the present and sustain a lively sense of the tradition, continuing habits of study are a professional imperative.

Amid the heavy pressures on many clergy, maintaining a study schedule is not easy. Opportunities for continuing education classes are widely available, and most clergy can find ways of taking advantage of some of them. Continuing education events should be carefully planned and judiciously limited. This enterprise too can become a path for evading regular parish responsibility, like overdoing furniture-making and tropical fish.

PRAYER

Attending to the spiritual life is another clergy responsibility. By most measures, ordained ministers admit to poor spiritual discipline. We spend little time at prayer. But more is to be said about that. Prayer is something other than a block of time.

The spiritual life is notoriously difficult to define. There are reflective, prayerful people who, like Brother Lawrence, fulfill outward responsibilities while still at prayer. They have learned to "pray without ceasing." Contrary to Brother Lawrence, however, full-time contemplatives and hermits do not make the best pastors. We need women and men who are also active in public tasks, fostering the communal, missional, and prayerful life of congregations.

At its base, prayer is more attitude, more inner disposition, than it is activity. It is the second sight that sees mystery in the commonplace, grace in the daily round, Holy Spirit present in human encounter. It is a second hearing that hears the Word in many of the words. It is awareness more than it is a unit of time; the capacity for wonder, grief, awe, joy, and compassion more than it is a form of pious exercise.

Yet the fact of the matter is that we need rhythms of explicit prayer; else that graced spirituality of prayerful awareness is all too unlikely to grow within us. We need punctuation marks to prevent busy professional lives from turning into awkward or meaningless run-on sentences of mere activity. We need moments of the hour, the day, and the week explicitly for prayer. We need seasons of retreat, times to ponder the Word, to meditate on the grace and righteousness of God.

To pray is to give attention to God receptively, expectantly, patiently. It is to turn away from and to discipline the "fat, relentless ego," to use Iris Murdock's phrase, the self-preoccupation that so distorts our vision and disposition toward the world. Most of us pray too actively, full of egocentric concern, full of petition, too impatient. Our call in prayer is to wait upon the Lord.

194

The spiritual life comprises much beyond such prayer, however. Therefore many pastors are gifted with strong religio-psychic health in spite of their limited time at devotional prayer and meditation. Their lives are fed by reflective study of the Scriptures in preparing for their preaching and teaching, by regular reading of theological journals, by compassionate counseling and spiritual direction, even by the reading of current social commentary with an inner ear attentive to the ways of God and the groaning needs of human liberation. These dimensions of our work and reflection do not always make for joy, but they counteract the shallowness and spiritual deadness that can afflict a thoughtless kind of ministry devoid of attention to transcendence and to Spirit.

The strength for ministry, like all human life, is a gift; the spiritual life remembers and builds on that. The gift comes with responsibility and a goal. Ephesians puts both well. As to personal responsibility, "Lead a life worthy of the calling to which you have been called, with all lowliness and meekness, with patience, forbearing one another in love, eager to maintain the unity of the Spirit in the bond of peace" (Eph. 4:1-3). As to vocational goal, the gifts to apostles, prophets, evangelists, pastors, and teachers are given "to equip the saints for the work of ministry, for building up the body of Christ," so that we may "grow up in every way into him who is the head, into Christ" (Eph. 4:12, 15).

Notes

1. David Riesman with Nathan Glazer and Reuel Denny, *The Lonely Crowd* (New York: Doubleday & Co., 1953), pp. 28-32.

2. Gaylord Noyce, "Phil Greenfield and the New Falls Church," ACT Case Bibliography #9-383-301, (Vandalia, Oh.: Association of Theological Schools, 1983).

3. Christian Church (Disciples of Christ), "My Code," p. 3.

11

A BRIEF POSTSCRIPT: "BUT IS THE MINISTRY A PROFESSION?"

This book has examined the practice of ministry through the lens of professional ethics. It has assumed both that this could be done and that it is appropriate to do so.

Some argue against these two assumptions. The most naive, of course, believe that since clergy mean well, the matter of ethics takes care of itself. Others suggest that the rubric "professional" demeans the ministry, or they argue that pastoral ministry is so unique a pursuit that it ought not to be squeezed into the category "profession."

One seminary's end-of-the-year evaluation form sent to pastors who had supervised field-education students inquired about evidence of "professional growth" on the part of the students. An angry scrawl marked out that question in the reply from a distinguished and able pastor: "The ministry is not a profession!"

AN AMBIGUOUS WORD

Professional is an ambiguous term. In a recent book, for example, Edward Farley discusses the fragmenting of theological education and what he defines as its "travail." He rehearses a history that has finally come to be—sadly, as he sees it—*professional* education. Once, he argues, the study of divinity meant "pious learning," a growth of wisdom in faith, "sapiential and personal knowledge."[1] Today theological education involves a cafeterialike offering of studies in specialized disciplines and an accumulation of professional skills. It is warped by a "clerical paradigm," a model of ministry understood as a set of clergy roles.

Many students experience a lack of coherence in preparing for ministry, to be sure. If it all seems to lack the coherence of the old divinity, we are tempted to blame this on the trend toward "professionalizing" the ministry, never mind a dozen other strands in the history of the church and the culture that might be equally responsible.

One response to Farley would run as follows. Presumably, if the ordained ministry *is* a profession, and if Farley's understanding of ministry is right, the richest and most thoughtful education for ministry would be what he calls "pious learning." It would be the "sapiential and personal knowledge" of God that he presents as far more central for the clergy than skill in pastoral counseling, administration, and homiletics. Becoming professional, in other words, is not the issue. The debate has to do with the *kind* of professional education we want.

In a classic essay, Talcott Parsons suggests that the most distinguishing mark of a profession is a special competence based on mastery of a realm of knowledge.[2] It is not a kit bag of skills. Farley deepens the kind of "knowledge" we need to achieve, and thereby offers important guidance for curriculum planners and theological faculty. His attack on the clerical paradigm need not be construed as an attack on understanding clergy as professionals in the truest, "professing" sense of the word.

Another kind of resistance to our undertaking arises from the ambiguity of the expression "professional ethics." Looking at ministry through this lens implies a common ground with the ethics of other professional groups whose codes are shot through with collusive self-interest. The clergy are to march to the beat of a different drummer, it would be said. Our cadences echo from scripture, with its servant image, for example, and that of the self-emptying Christ of Philippians, and with the command to take up the cross.

Andrew Manson, the young physician in A. J. Cronin's *The Citadel*, calls a medical board "slaves of professional etiquette, [not] disciples of medicine. . . . All they are concerned about is ethics . . . . There's no concern at all for suffering humanity." Jacques Ellul contrasts vocation and profession as "a total divorce between what society unceasingly asks of us and God's will. Service to God cannot be written into a profession."[3]

The arguments go on. Ivan Illich recently wrote of a "techno-fascism" that we may suffer as the experts in their professional "cartels" treat so many human dilemmas as "problems" and "needs" to which they—and only they— have the answers. *Disabling Professions*,[4] he calls his book. Another book, already cited, is written by a highly committed and thoughtful group of Mennonite authors. Its title: *Perils of Professionalism*. "We are convinced," say the editors, "that at the bottom of the professional drama is the issue of social power."[5]

Much of the behavior of professional groups can be understood as a reach for power. Nonetheless, the protests of professional groups that they are service-oriented do not necessarily make for outright hypocrisy. Hypocrisy is feigned virtue, conscious deceit; many professional groups partly believe what they say about service. They believe that their concern for professional regulation will protect the public. The clergy hold that view of themselves too.

Moreover, these professional groups are partly right. A valid concern for authority arises in any social order. Conflicting claims must be adjudicated, goods and services coordinated, cultural institutions established. All organization, be it ever so nonhierarchical, involves authority. But "authority" can also be a smokescreen behind which those in power maintain illegitimate control and keep others dependent instead of free and growing. "Beware of the scribes, who like to go about in long robes," said Jesus (Luke 20:46).

By what authority are you acting? the professional priests and lawyers asked the upstart from Nazareth (Luke 20:2). Gamaliel had the more wholesome view: tolerance for the new grassroots Christian movement (Acts 5:35-39).

"PROFESSIONAL" MORE POSITIVELY DEFINED

Few laypeople will quibble when we call an ordained minister from one of the mainline churches a professional. This usage is a sociological and linguistic convenience. Typically, a professional is a member of a company of practitioners who have a commonly agreed upon threshold of education and training, who maintain standards of entry into and of minimal ethical standards within the practice, and who are presumed to serve goals beyond their own self-interest. The three traditional such "learned" professions were law, medicine, and ordained ministry.

With modernization and the wide proliferation of special occupational pursuits, the "professions" have multiplied. Many new groups meet all the criteria—biochemists, engineers, certified public accountants. Other groups regularly endeavor to promote themselves into professional status—beauticians, bookkeepers, office equipment maintenance personnel. Remembering to counteract our self-deception, and holding Christian convictions about the respect owed every person and every person's work when it is responsibly pursued, we can have little quarrel with this particular expansion of English usage, inconvenient as it is to those who want to write about or educate in the traditional professions.

What we can and must stress, however, is something rooted in the etymology of the word *professional*. The word evolves from Latin roots having to do with making a public declaration, *pro fateri*. The most common early use relates to making a vow, as by monks upon entering their order. It carries with it not so much a claim to knowledge and skill as a profession of commitment. Culturally, the modern professions trace their line back to the medieval clergy.

The reason that *professional* takes on negative connotations has more to do with Bernard Shaw's view of professions as conspiracies against the laity than with this etymology. *Professional* can now be used as a term of disparagement. *The New Century Dictionary* (published in 1934) cites this usage as follows: "Making a business or trade of something not properly to be regarded as a business (as a *professional* politician; *professional* beauty)." *Professional* has lost much of its sense of commitment to value and service. As the word has evolved, it has come to relate more to the matter of expertise than to public declaration of selfless intention.

Yet *professional* is far from a useless word when applied to personal values and responsibility. Consider briefly how the word differs from another: *technician*—a word we have used a number of times in foregoing chapters. Without drawing ironclad distinctions, it is still easy to uncover different connotations of the words.

CATEGORY	PROFESSIONAL	TECHNICIAN
Scope of concern	Broad	Narrow
Authority	Self-disciplined	Directed by a superior
Range of Information	Integrates information for making judgment	Follows a manual
Object of Concern	Persons, personal values	Things, materials

Clearly, some lawyers, physicians, and architects (and clergy) tend to do their work a little more like technicians than others of their professional companions, and some laboratory technicians, receptionists, and mechanics, because of the style of their own work and their personal character, are more "professional" as they do a technician's job.

Sociologically, the ministry qualifies as a profession. People who resist using the word for pastors are making a theological point. Is the ministry rightly understood as a profession, they ask, when we are talking about practicing theology and announcing the Good News of God? The question begs clarification because it mixes categories. We run into the same kind of mix elsewhere, of course. For example, we can ask, Is the church—to borrow a sociological term—a voluntary association? Empirically the church is just that, a voluntary association of the religious type. Theologically, however, the church is not that voluntary; it is something else. There is a necessity here. We are brought into the church, as we say, by the constraint of Christ and by the grace of God. Is the ministry a profession? Yes, and no, similarly.

INSTITUTION AND ORDAINED MINISTRY

One of the wrongheaded reasons that some argue against the "professionalizing" of the ministry stems from a feeling that the minister is not an institutional person. Emil Brunner, in *The Misunderstanding of the Church*[6] urged us to think of the church as a movement rather than as an institution. And institutions, not movements, appoint professional leadership. The term *institution* commonly connotes stagnation for many of us, but this idea is belied, or ought to be, by our vision of the church in mission and of the church *semper reformanda*. "The church exists by mission as a fire exists by burning," we have said. To be merely a functionary in an organization plopped down on the landscape, even—especially—as an unusually competent and "professional" minister, who possesses all the needed skills for such a role—*that* definition of ordained ministry is not for you and me. Better to say we are part of a movement than occupants of an office, if that is all it means.

Brunner's criticism keeps us alert to the deadened institutionalism that forgets God's moving Spirit that is, as we believe, at work in the church. Yet we cannot avoid the empirical realities and the theological imperatives that make of the church an institution. Docetism was pronounced heresy a long time ago.

The richest use of the words *profession* and *professional* has more to do with the character of the person than with the skills of performance. This emphasis is analogous to the emphasis now placed on character, as opposed to rules, in theological ethics.[7] One congregation, as it began searching for a new pastor, expressed this concern so well that its description of what it sought in a new pastor is worth quoting at length. (The search went on in days before our concerns for inclusive language.)

> Fundamental to all else, the individual will exhibit the kind of personal freedom which stems from his knowing who he is, and that he is his own man. He will be free to *be* who he is, able to affirm his strengths and acknowledge his limitations. He will be free to share *himself* and not merely his ideas and advice. He will be able to live with his own anxiety and to cope with anger and frustration.
>
> He will have the freedom which goes with a capacity for flexibility, for adaptability, for sitting loose to experimentation and change. He will know how to cut himself away from practices of tradition which have become sanctified simply because they are "traditional." At the same time, he will be free from compulsive addictions to novelty for its own sake . . . .
>
> He will have the kind of freedom which comes with being an adept administrator. He will not get hung up, sidetracked, or trapped in the how, when, and where of getting a job done . . . .
>
> The minister will be someone whose stance and sense of direction indicates a thorough grounding in the biblical and theological heritage of the faith . . . .

The man will be sensitive to a wide spectrum of attitudes, ideas, and feelings represented in the membership. He will be a ready, patient listener and learner, and will deal creatively with conflict. He will bring to all his relationships a genuine pastoral sense, marked by real caring and compassion for all temperaments and mind-sets.

Here is a plea for personal strength and spirit, a plea for the gifts (and requirements) of ministry well beyond its "skills." Here, too, I would submit, is a solid description of a professional.

The late Urban T. Holmes ended his long study, *The Future Shape of Ministry*, with an argument that the pastor-priest be both professional and 'charismatic,' institutional, and spirit-filled. In stressing the uniqueness of the ordained pastor, however, Holmes made too much of the 'liminality' of the priest, the shamanistic mysteriousness of the pastor's call to evoke spiritual consciousness and growth.

I would define the charismatic person as someone to whom is given a quality of character that is contagious, spontaneous, mysterious, and essentially eschatological. . . . The professional person I would define as someone who on the basis of a body of knowledge has developed skills to achieve in his relations with others a predictable end. . . . The heart of the Christian ministry is its charismatic, liminal quality. . . . [T]he power of Christian ministry lies in the sacramental person.[8]

In his strenuous emphasis to that side, Holmes flew in the face of much of the Reformation's legitimate concern to emphasize that all Christians are called to Christ's ministry and that God's grace, not the spiritual leadership of anyone, saves us. Holmes seemed to rule out much of what humility forces us to say about our own ordination to the role of leadership in the church. Essentially, we are just like other mortals, sinners blessed—and cursed—with clay feet. For the Protestant, at least, emphasis on unique 'spiritual' qualities supposedly possessed by the priesthood (and *not* the laity?) leads to a Pandora's box of theological and moral confusion.

The professional issue is well put in one of the best brief books on ministry, Henri Nouwen's *Creative Ministry*. Nouwen's subtitle is "Beyond Professionalism." "Professionalism" in this case refers to the perfunctory exercise of ministry tasks—counseling by the rules and without compassion or much insight; preaching without spirit; teaching that tells information without evoking learning and understanding; administering that doesn't inspire participation; leading liturgy in a way that is mostly "going through the motions."

Nouwen does not imply for a moment that these other gifts are somehow more present in the ordained than in all Christian "ministers"—the laity, but he urges that clergy attend to their development as faithful persons. "[S]piritual guidance and professional formation are . . . so closely related that any separation will, in the long run, do harm to both aspects of the daily life of the man or woman who wants to be of Christian service to his [sic] fellow man."[9] Of teaching, for example, Nouwen writes that it "becomes ministry when the teacher moves beyond the transference of knowledge and is willing to offer his own life experience to his student so that . . . new liberating insight and real learning can take place."[10] Likewise, in preaching, counseling, and organizing, and in liturgical leadership, Nouwen stresses the need for an analogous investment of the minister's caring self to complement the exercise of competence.

IN SUM: COMMITMENT AND COMPETENCE

To revert to etymology, the true professional is one who lives into his or her work on the basis of a professed and competent personal intention, monitored and disciplined by the guild. In the case of the clergy, this intention is to be a commitment toward God, toward the church, and toward the world. The end in view is the increase of faith, taken in its broadest meaning, with diverse ramifications in cultural and institutional life.

All this is not to say that the work of the ordained ministry is impossible to delineate in intelligible language, according to the tasks of ministry. It is to assign to such a list some activities beyond communicating, organizing, counseling, preaching, and teaching. We may add, for example, such basic competencies in the work as these: the ability to maintain and enlarge a personal appropriation of Scripture, and the way its role in the church provides a fundamental critique of the culture; the ability to interpret this in the midst of congregational life so that others, too, catch the vision; the ability to evoke in others an understanding of and commitment to the church insofar as it serves the mission of God in the world, and to evoke in others a loyal opposition to the church insofar as it does not; the ability to be not only a good personal counselor but also a spiritual director or "soul-friend"; the ability to recognize in oneself the same human frailties and foibles that are in others, and therefore to work well alongside professional and Christian companions without clerical pretense and hypocrisy.

These abilities belong to an order of competence that is different from and "beyond" the usual list of professional skills like exegesis and organizing, of client-centered counseling and liturgical reading.

APPROACHES TO PASTORAL ETHICS

Serving God's vision for the world, we believe, involves refining and tempering the mission of the church. Toughening the church's mission involves strengthening the leadership of the churches, lay and ordained. In a time of no little confusion, one useful method in that process can be an analysis of professional responsibilities of the clergy.

We might have taken other routes. We might have taken an empirical approach, surveying the codes of ethics adopted by clergy groups and denominational judicatories, or simply describing the practices of present-day clergy.

We might have taken a historical tack, inquiring into the stated norms and self-understandings of clergy through the centuries of the Christian era. We could have looked at guiding images of ministry from the past: the sacramental person,[11] the pastoral ruler, the evangelist, the interpreter of the word. These motifs have been usefully described in *The Ministry in Historical Perspectives* (edited by Niebuhr and Williams). We could then have proceeded to unearth more particularly the professional and ethical shape of ministry in those several epochs. Thomas Oden, in *Pastoral Theology*, focuses on the norms in the older tradition, always preferring a source in the church fathers, if it is available, in contrast to a more modern one, as he works his way through issues and perspectives in ministry.[12] Neither book pulls out professional ethics as an explicit focus.

Our approach has reflected on varied pastoral responsibilities in our present culture. We have worked from quandaries that arise for the conscientious minister, from concerns of the faith, *and* from a conceptual framework for professional ethics. Ethics is always a bridging enterprise. If Paul Tillich believes theology must use a method of correlation, far more is this true with ethics. What shall we do? we ask—in this case or that case. Why? When obligations conflict, how shall we sort them out?—in this case or that case. And again, Why?

The most fundamental questions, however, go beneath that. They have to do with our self-understanding as servants of God, and of our understanding of the way the church is to serve the *missio dei* in a world society at this stage of its evolution. There can be no simple rule book, not without deadening our sense of ministry. Ministry is not a technician's assignment. Rather we must ground our service in faithful prayer and Godward study, seasoned by continuing conversation with the world, and among church people of all stripes and responsibilities. Given that multivectored set of concerns, both our ministry and the witness of the church can be renewed by the unstinting grace of God that we have come to know in Christ Jesus.

Yes, the ordained ministry is a profession. It is also a gift, and a vocation, a calling. By holding on to some ambivalence about the word *profession*, we can move toward a deeper understanding of our work. By that ambivalence we point to the commitments that must ground all good professional ethics. God willing, we shall thereby be better pastors for the church, and also be of assistance to others in their own Christian callings in the world.

Notes

1. Edward Farley, *Theologia: The Fragmentation and Unity of Theological Education* (Philadelphia: Fortress Press, 1983), p. xi.

2. Talcott Parsons, "The Professions and Social Structure," *Social Forces* 17 (1939): 459-67.

3. Jacques Ellul, "Work and Calling," in *Callings*, by W. D. Campbell and J. Y. Halloway (New York: Paulist Press, 1974), p. 33.

4. Ivan Illich, et al., *Disabling Professions* (London: Marion Boyars, 1977).

5. Kraybill and Good, *Perils*, p. 8.

6. Emil Brunner, *The Misunderstanding of the Church* (London: Lutterworth Press, 1952).

7. See, e.g., Hauerwas, *Community of Character*, ch. 7.

8. Urban T. Holmes, III, *The Future Shape of Ministry* (New York: Seabury Press, 1971), p. 248.

9. Henri Nouwen, *Creative Ministry* (New York: Doubleday & Co., 1971), p. xvi.

10. Ibid., p. 110-11.

11. Urban T. Holmes, III, *The Future Shape of Ministry* (New York: Seabury Press, 1971).

12. Oden, *Pastoral Theology*.

BIBLIOGRAPHY

Books

Baptism, Eucharist, and Ministry, Faith and Order Paper No. 111. Geneva: World Council of Churches, 1982.

Biersdorf, John, ed. *Creating an Intentional Ministry.* Nashville: Abingdon, 1976.

Bok, Sissela. *Lying.* New York: Random House, 1978.

————. *Secrets.* New York: Random House, 1982.

The Book of Order. New York: General Assembly, United Presbyterian Church in the United States of America, 1981–1982.

Browning, Don. *Religious Ethics and Pastoral Care.* Philadelphia: Fortress Press, 1983.

————. *The Moral Context of Pastoral Care.* Philadelphia: Westminster Press, 1976.

Brueggemann, Walter. *The Prophetic Imagination.* Philadelphia: Fortress Press, 1978.

Brunner, Emil. *The Misunderstanding of the Church.* London: Lutterworth Press, 1952.

Campbell, Dennis M. *Doctors, Lawyers, Ministers: Christian Ethics in Professional Practice.* Nashville: Abingdon, 1982.

Campbell, Ernest Q., and Thomas F. Pettigrew. *Christians in Racial Crisis.* Washington, D.C.: Public Affairs Press, 1959.

Campbell, Thomas C., and Gary B. Reierson. *The Gift of Administration.* Philadelphia: Westminster Press, 1981.

Carroll, Jackson W. *Ministry as Reflective Practice*. Washington, D.C.: The Alban Institute, 1986.

Clebsch, William R., and Charles R. Jaekle. *Pastoral Care in Historical Perspective*. New York: Jason Aaronson, 1964.

Cone, James H. *My Soul Looks Back*. Nashville: Abingdon, 1982.

Craddock, Fred B. *Overhearing the Gospel*. Nashville: Abingdon, 1978.

Dittes, James E. *Minister on the Spot*. Philadelphia: Pilgrim Press, 1970.

Dulles, Avery. *Models of the Church*. New York: Doubleday & Co., 1974.

Elliott, Philip. *The Sociology of the Professions*. New York: Herder & Herder, 1972.

Farley, Edward. *Theologia: The Fragmentation and Unity of Theological Education*. Philadelphia: Fortress Press, 1983.

Fichter, Joseph H. *Priest and People*. New York: Sheed and Ward, 1965.

Firet, Jacob. *Dynamics in Pastoring*. Grand Rapids, Mich.: Wm. B. Eerdmans Publishing Co., 1986.

Fowler, James. *Stages of Faith*. San Francisco: Harper & Row, Publishers, 1981.

Fray, Harold R., Jr. *Conflict and Change in the Church*. Boston: Pilgrim Press, 1969.

Friedson, Eliot, ed. *The Professions and Their Prospects*. Beverly Hills, Cal.: Sage Publications, 1973.

General Assembly, United Presbyterian Church in the United States of America. *The Book of Order*. New York: 1981–1982.

Gilligan, Carol. *In a Different Voice*. Cambridge, Mass.: Harvard University Press, 1982.

Glasse, James D. *Profession: Minister*. Nashville/New York: Abingdon Press, 1968.

Goldman, Alan H. *The Moral Foundations of Professional Ethics*. Totowa, N.J.: Rowman and Littlefield, 1980.

Gumper, Lindell L. *Legal Issues in the Practice of Ministry*. Birmingham, Mich.: Psychological Studies and Consultation Program, 1981.

Gurin, G., J. Veroff, and S. Feld. *Americans View Their Mental Health*. New York: Basic Books, 1960.

Hadden, Jeffrey. *The Gathering Storm in the Churches*. New York: Doubleday & Co., 1969.

Harmon, Nolan B., Jr. *Ministerial Ethics and Etiquette.* Nashville: Cokesbury Press, 1928.

Harris, John C. *Stress, Power and Ministry.* Washington, D.C.: The Alban Institute, 1977.

Hauerwas, Stanley. *A Community of Character.* Notre Dame, Ind.: University of Notre Dame Press, 1981.

Holifield, E. Brooks. *A History of Pastoral Care in America.* Nashville: Abingdon Press, 1983.

Holmes, Urban T., III. *The Future Shape of Ministry.* New York: Seabury Press, 1971.

Hough, Joseph C., Jr., and John B. Cobb, Jr. *Christian Identity and Theological Education.* Chico, Cal.: Scholars Press, 1985.

Illich, Ivan, et al. *Disabling Professions.* London: Marion Boyars, 1977.

Johnson, Terence J. *Professions and Power.* London: Macmillan Publishers, 1972.

Kelley, Dean. *Why Conservative Churches Are Growing: A Study in Sociology of Religion.* New York: Harper & Row, Publishers, 1972.

Knowles, Malcolm. *The Adult Learner.* Houston: Gulf Publishing Co., 1973.

Kohlberg, Lawrence. *The Philosophy of Moral Development.* San Francisco: Harper & Row, Publishers, 1981.

Kraybill, Donald B., and Phyllis Pellman Good, eds. *Perils of Professionalism: Essays on Christian Faith and Professionalism.* Scottdale, Pa.: Herald Press, 1982.

Leech, Kenneth. *Soul Friend.* San Francisco: Harper & Row, Publishers, 1980.

Leiffer, Murray H. *Changing Expectations and Ethics in the Professional Ministry.* Evanston: Garrett Theological Seminary, 1969.

Levinson, Daniel J. *The Seasons of a Man's Life.* New York: Ballantine Books, 1978.

Lewis, Sinclair. *Elmer Gantry.* New York: Harcourt, Brace & Co., 1927.

Lynn, Kenneth S., ed. *The Professions in America.* Boston: Beacon Press, 1963.

MacIntyre, Alasdair. *After Virtue.* Notre Dame, Ind.: University of Notre Dame Press, 1981.

Maloney, H. Newton, Thomas L. Needham, and Samuel Southard. *Clergy Malpractice.* Philadelphia: Westminster Press, 1986.

Marty, Martin. *The Public Church.* New York: Crossroad Books, 1981.

May, William F. *The Physician's Covenant*. Philadelphia: Westminster Press, 1983.

McKown, Delos Banning. *With Faith and Fury*. Buffalo: Prometheus Books, 1985.

McNeill, John T. *A History of the Cure of Souls*. New York: Harper & Brothers, 1951.

Menninger, Karl. *Whatever Became of Sin?* New York: Hawthorn Books, 1973.

Mueller, Frederick F., and Hugh Hartshorne. *Ethical Dilemmas of Ministers*. New York: Charles Scribner's Sons, 1937.

Niebuhr, H. Richard. *The Purpose of the Church and Its Ministry*. New York: Harper & Brothers, 1956.

Niebuhr, H. Richard, and Daniel D. Williams, eds. *The Ministry in Historical Perspectives*. San Francisco: Harper & Brothers, 1956, rev. ed., 1983.

Nouwen, Henri. *Creative Ministry*. New York: Doubleday & Co., 1971.

Oates, Wayne. *The Christian Pastor*. Philadelphia: Westminster Press, 1963.

Oden, Thomas C. *Pastoral Theology: Essentials of Ministry*. San Francisco: Harper & Row, Publishers, 1983.

Omeara, Thomas Franklin, o.p. *Theology of Ministry*. New York: Paulist Press, 1983.

Palmer, Parker. *The Company of Strangers: Christians and the Renewal of America's Public Life*. New York: Crossroad, 1981.

Paul, Robert S. *Ministry*. Grand Rapids: Wm. B. Eerdmans Publishing Co., 1965.

Potter, Ralph. *War and Moral Discourse*. Atlanta: John Knox Press, 1969.

Ramsey, Paul. *Who Speaks for the Church?* Nashville/New York: Abingdon Press, 1967.

Riesman, David, with Nathan Glazer and Reuel Denney. *The Lonely Crowd*. New York: Doubleday & Co., 1953.

Russell, Letty. *The Future of Partnership*. Philadelphia: Westminster Press, 1979.

Schoen, Donald. *The Reflective Practitioner: How Professionals Think in Action*. New York: Basic Books, 1983.

Scott, Donald. *From Office to Profession*. Philadelphia: University of Pennsylvania Press, 1978.

Shelp, Earle E., and Ronald H. Sunderland, eds. *The Pastor as Prophet*. New York: Pilgrim Press, 1985.

Smith, Donald P. *Clergy in the Cross Fire.* Philadelphia: Westminster Press, 1978.

Thompson, T. K., ed. *Stewardship in Contemporary Life.* New York: Association Press, 1965.

Thornton, Edward. *Theology and Pastoral Counseling.* Englewood Cliffs, N.J.: Prentice Hall, 1964.

Thornton, Martin. *Pastoral Theology: A Reorientation.* London: S.P.C.K., 1961.

Thurneysen, Eduard. *A Theology of Pastoral Care.* Richmond: John Knox Press, 1962.

Tiemann, William Harold. *The Right to Silence.* Richmond: John Knox Press, 1964.

Tupper, Charles B. *Called in Honor.* St. Louis: Bethany Press, 1949.

United Presbyterian Church in the U.S.A. *Presbyterian Law for the Local Church.* New York: UPUSA, 1981.

Vera, Hernan. *The Professionalization and Professionalism of Catholic Priests.* Gainesville: University Presses of Florida, 1982.

Weidman, Judith L., ed. *Women Ministers: How Women Are Re-defining Traditional Roles.* San Francisco: Harper & Row, Publishers, 1981.

West, Cornel. *Prophesy Deliverance.* Philadelphia: Westminster Press, 1982.

Whitehead, James D. and Evelyn E. Whitehead. *Method in Ministry.* New York: Seabury Press, 1980.

Winter, Gibson. *The Suburban Captivity of the Churches.* New York: Doubleday & Co., 1961.

Articles

Bok, Sissela. "The Limits of Confidentiality." *Hastings Center Report* (February 1983).

Campbell, Dennis M. "The Ordained Ministry as a Profession." *Quarterly Review* III:2 (Summer 1983).

Carroll, Jackson W. "The Professional Model of Ministry—Is It Worth Saving?" *Theological Education* XXI (Spring 1985).

Davis, Michael. "Conflict of Interest." *Business and Professional Ethics Journal* I:4 (Summer 1982).

Ellul, Jacques. "Work and Calling," in *Callings*, by W. D. Campbell and J. Y. Halloway. New York: Paulist Press, 1974.

Fishburn, Janet F. "Male Clergy Adultery as Vocational Confusion." *The Christian Century* (September 15-22, 1982).
Fishburn, Janet F., and Neill Q. Hamilton. "Seminary Education Tested by Praxis." *The Christian Century* (February 1-8, 1984).
Fry, Clyde C. "Ethics for Clergy in the Hospital Setting." Report to the Academy of Parish Clergy, Annual Meeting (1982).

Gustafson, James. " 'Professions' as 'Callings.' " *The Social Service Review* 56 (December 1982).
———. "The Ethics of Promotion: Stewardship as Promotion," in *Stewardship in Contemporary Life*, by T. K. Thompson, ed. New York: Association Press, 1965.
———. "The Minister as Moral Counselor." *Proceedings*, Association for Professional Education for Ministry (1982).

Hulme, William E. "Pastors' Salaries." *The Christian Ministry* (November 1985).
Hyers, Conrad. "The Comic Vision in a Tragic World." *The Christian Century* (April 20, 1983).

Lee, Ronald R. "Referral as an Act of Pastoral Care." *The Journal of Pastoral Care* (September 1976).

Mabon, Joan. "My Friend, the Former Pastor . . . ," *Action Information* (Alban Institute, 4125 Nebraska Ave., N.W., Washington, D.C., 20016) (April 1980).

Noyce, Gaylord. "Phil Greenfield and the New Falls Church." ACT Case Bibliography, #9-383-301. Vandalia, Oh.: Association of Theological Schools, 1983.

Parsons, Talcott. "The Professions and Social Structure," *Social Forces* 17:4 (May 1939).
Posey, Lawton. "All Rights Reserved." *The Christian Ministry* (January 1983).

Spong, John Shelby. "Can the Church Bless Divorce?" *The Christian Century* (November 28, 1984).
Steckel, Clyde. "The Ministry as Profession and Calling." *Word and World* I:4 (Fall 1981).
"Sexual Contact by Pastors and Pastoral Counselors in Professional Relationships." Seattle: Washington Association of Churches, 1984.

INDEX